WELLNESS THRU LIFE'S LESSONS

Tyneisah Barnes

ISBN: 1545133727
ISBN 13: 9781545133729

In remembrance of my grandmother Audrey Clarissa Barnes.

CONTENTS

ACKNOWLEDGMENTS

I could have written this book sooner, but I was still on my journey to happiness. Life has a way of giving you exactly what you need to start the next chapter. I was fortunate to have been presented with some great people, to whom I would like to show my eternal gratitude.

First and foremost, I would like to thank God for giving me a sound purpose. I also thank my parents, Thomas and Bernetta Barnes, who have helped me to be the woman I am today. They have uplifted me and encouraged me along this interesting journey. Thanks to my brothers, Jarelle, Marcus, and Justin Barnes. Jarelle (a.k.a. Dimp), whom I call my big brother, you have been a great support system in my dreams. Never give up on your music career. Marcus, you have been a great listener and adviser as I was going through troubled relationships. Continue on your path of artistic creations. Justin, my little brother, you have been my light in times of darkness from the time you were born. Make the difference in the justice system that I know you can. Thanks to my sister-in-law, Tawanda Barnes, for being the sister I never had and for sharing business and personal advice. My best friends, Rosie Martin, Jimmese Cupid, Kimberly Perry, and Vanessa Web, thank you for always listening to me. Thanks to my cousins Natina Davis and Darlene Brown for giving me sound advice as I started to mature into a business-oriented woman; my aunt Thomacina Baylor for connecting me to an author who gave me tips and directed me onto an organized path to create this book; and my photographer, Michael Secrecy, for being so patient with me and for your great work in creating a successful book cover. To all the people I have encountered along my journey, thank you!

INTRODUCTION

Looking back on my life, I feel very accomplished. I am many things: the owner of Ty's Tropics, a life coach, a massage therapist, and now an author. The road to my success wasn't easy. In fact, it was extremely difficult. I never thought the end results would be what they are. When I was in my twenties, my dream was to become an animal behaviorist, but as we all know, as we grow, our dreams can sometimes change. The struggles I faced in life enhanced and fueled my growth and gave me strength. This is my story.

LESSON 1

A BIRTH OR REBIRTH STARTS
A NEW BEGINNING

It was the winter of 1981 when a teen mom-to-be was rushed to the emergency room for delivery. Angie was a tall, slim girl whose life was about to change in more ways than one. Her boyfriend, Shawn, a five-foot-ten-inch boy with a light-brown complexion and strong stature, was driving, and Leana, Angie's mother, was on the passenger side, while Angie was in the middle. Labor pains increased the closer they got to the hospital. It was five in the morning, still dark and cold. Leana urged Shawn to move faster. They came to a red light, and she said, "Go through the light. She's in labor, Shawn!" Shawn sped up and went straight through the red light. He made two quick lefts, and there they were at the front of the hospital building.

Leana jumped from the car and raced inside, saying, "My daughter's in labor! Quick, quick!" A nurse at the front desk dressed in blue scrubs rushed to retrieve a wheelchair.

The hospital had an eerie feel to it—not the usual warm and inviting feel. The tiles were dusty and slightly worn down. The hallways were narrow, and scents of earth and nursing home filled the hallways.

Angie's pains intensified as the nurse wheeled her to a room, where she was asked to change into a gown and lie on a table. Her mother and a tall, thin nurse with short, dark hair helped her get on the table. By this time, the pains had intensified to the point where Angie was yelling. One nurse, a nasty older redhead, said, "Oh, calm down. It's not that bad."

Angie said, "Yes, it is."

What was interesting was that there was a woman screaming louder than Angie, and she was a much older woman. She was saying, "Get this thing out of me!"

Once they gave Angie the epidural, it was smooth sailing. She didn't feel anything after that. When the doctor came in to examine her, she said, "It's time to have this baby." They grabbed the proper tools, placed her feet in the stirrups, and began to tell her to push. Angie was pushing, but they had given her too much of the epidural, and she was completely numb. All she was doing was making grunting sounds; she couldn't feel anything from the waist down. At this time the doctor instructed the nurse and Leana to help her push and bear down. There were several pushes, and out came her baby. Angie was excited, but when she saw all the blood and creamy white substance smeared all over her child, all she wanted was for them to clean up her baby. Once the baby was cleaned to near perfection, the nurses placed her into Angie's arms.

Shawn was outside in the waiting room, pacing the floor and wrestling with the worry "Is she OK? Is the baby OK?" He couldn't bear another minute of this agony of not knowing. He eventually called his mother to inform her that the baby was on the way. His mother, Clara, was thrilled and tried to reassure him that everything would be OK. He knew that his life was going to change in a matter of minutes. Then a short nurse came to retrieve Shawn so he could meet his little girl. He was so overjoyed! He couldn't imagine how the joy of seeing his baby girl would make him feel.

Next, he signed the birth certificate, and the nurse noted the time of birth, which was 6:15 a.m., and the weight, which was seven pounds six ounces.

The young teen mother marveled at what she had brought into this world. She named her daughter Terri. She was overjoyed and a little frightened at the responsibilities that lay in front her, but in that very moment, all she saw was her blessing from God. Angie had heard of miracles but never thought she would see one in the eyes of her newborn baby girl.

Shawn, her high school sweetheart, was excited as well, and both new parents knew they had a major responsibility. Shawn had to step up to the plate and make sure he had adequate income. For a while, he'd worked with his family picking tobacco and doing little side jobs, which was OK when it was just him, but now he had a family to support. Two weeks after the baby's birth, he received word that he could become an employee of a retreat home located in Maryland.

Angie had to step into womanhood early and without hesitation, but it was very natural for her. It was as if she had instructions mapped out in her head, but she was prepared—oh, she did her research. A baby, in most cases, forces parents to apply themselves in ways they never thought they could. It forces them to think outside themselves and simply grow up.

Taking the baby home was the fun part. When the young couple arrived home, there were tons of family members all waiting and very enthusiastic to see the new addition to the family. The baby was the first grandchild on Shawn's side, and Shawn's mother, Clara, was tickled to death to see the baby. Angie grew rather attached to Clara, who was funny but didn't bite her tongue. She would speak her mind and crack a joke in the same breath. Clara stood about five feet six inches and had brown eyes and reddish-brown hair. She made sure that Angie and the baby were taken care of. The bond between the two grew. Clara loved Angie as if she was one of her own. She was a great cook and made some of the best meals. She knew how to compose a feast out of the least amount of food. She and her husband, Jack, had raised five boys with huge appetites. They also had a baby girl who passed just a few months after her birth. So even though Angie wasn't Clara's own child, she did perceive her as one of her own.

The two would prepare wood for the fire, cook meals, go on road trips to the supermarket, and sit up talking all night. During this time, Angie and Shawn started to go through many different changes. Shawn still wanted to be free, and sometimes he would hang out with his friends and leave Angie for days, because he was too busy wanting to still have fun. Angie looked to Clara and her baby for comfort. At times she found herself a little depressed and perplexed about whether this relationship was for her. She loved Shawn and wanted to make it work. She couldn't just walk away, so she hung in there and proceeded full force ahead despite his disappearing acts. They spent a substantial amount of time at Shawn's parents' house in Newburg, Maryland.

Three years later, Angie found herself pregnant again, and this time she had a baby boy with jet-black hair and Asian eyes. She named him Darnell. Shawn was extremely happy to welcome his son home. At this time Angie and Shawn were still living with relatives, sometimes with her family and other times with his. The couple had two young kids and knew that they needed a place of their own, but how would they get it?

LESSON 2

GROWTH CAN ONLY OCCUR WHEN YOU CREATE SPACE FOR IT

I t was one cold and gloomy day in February of 1984. Angie and the children, Terri and Darnell, were all sitting on the couch watching the children's favorite cartoons when they heard the muffled sound of an engine. Terri, age three at this point, looked out the window and said, "Daddy's home."

Angie went to the door with one-month-old Darnell in her arms, and she and the kids greeted Shawn with hugs. She noticed that something was different about him. He'd come home from work with excitement in his eyes and was unusually energetic. She noticed his overly eager look, and his smile that seemed to be frozen in time. So she asked him, "What are you up to?"

He replied, "How about we go for a ride?" He had a huge surprise for Angie that would completely shock her.

So they gathered the children together in their '84 Honda Civic and ventured down the country roads of King George, Virginia. Angie had started to get a little annoyed because it seemed they were just riding around burning gas. She finally said, "OK, what is it that you have up your sleeve, Shawn?"

He responded, "You will see. As matter of fact, close your eyes, woman."

The car started to turn left, and then right, and then another left, and then it came to an abrupt stop. She felt the jerk of the car and asked, "Can I open my eyes now?"

It was time for the surprise to be revealed. Shawn said, "OK, Angie, you can open your eyes."

She looked up and said, "What is this? Is this what I think it is?" They were standing in front of a two-bedroom mobile home with blue-and-white trim. It was just enough space for the kids to play and perfect for a couple just starting out.

Shawn said, "Yes, baby, all ours."

She could barely contain the tears of joy that welled up in her eyes. The tears began to slide down her cheeks. Shawn wiped her eyes while he embraced her with comforting arms. She asked when they could move in, and he said in two days. That evening, Angie quickly gathered up all their belongings, getting all the clothes and toys packed and ready to go. She was so excited! This was the most joy she had experienced since the birth of her children. It was time to create the life she had always wanted.

Settling into Nesting Acres seemed to be quite nice. It was a very family-oriented mobile-home park, and it was filled with lots of familiar faces. It housed about fifty trailers at the time, but that number soon grew.

The young family continued to grow, and four years after they moved into the mobile home, Angie gave birth to another son. His hair was dark brown and wavy, and he had chubby cheeks. She called him Jarvis. Shawn was extremely excited that he had two sons to continue the last name. The family needed one last thing to solidify it, and Shawn knew exactly what that was.

One Christmas morning, when the kids were all opening gifts, Shawn said to Angie, "Open your gift, honey."

Angie was very excited for her gift. She had wanted a radio/cassette player for Christmas, but when she opened the package, it was a set of dishes. Shocked but still trying to show her appreciation, she looked at Shawn and said, "Oh, that's nice. Thanks, honey."

He looked down into the box and said, "Angie, did you see the other gift you have in the box?"

She said, "I did. It's nice. Thanks again."

Shawn then reached into the bottom, and there was a ring box. He got down on one knee and said, "Would you do me the honor of being my wife?" Angie had an interesting sense of humor, and she laughed and said yes. The kids all were excited and jumping for joy—their parents were tying the knot.

Two years later, on August 18, 1990, Angie married Shawn. It was a beautiful ceremony, held in a lodge in little old King George, Virginia. Everything was decorated with black, white, and red. More than one hundred guests witnessed the union between high school sweethearts.

LESSON 3

AS CHILDREN, WE ARE INNOCENT AND FRAGILE TO OUR ENVIRONMENT

Growing up in little old King George, Virginia, I wasn't really exposed to a lot other than the country roads, the large farms, the wooded areas, and the beach, which at the time was the best part of King George to me. The adventures on the beach consisted of my mother, aunt, uncle, cousin, and myself bringing lunch and drinks and piling in a station wagon. Those were the days. King George didn't have a lot, but what we had seemed like the best.

As a child I was filled with energy, and I wanted to explore things. I loved to entertain and put on shows and even sing for my family. We had family who would come over during the holidays, and my little cousins and I would put on shows that would captivate the whole family's attention. This one particular song that I would sing was by Tina Turner, "What's Love Got to Do with It?" My brother Darnell and I sang many songs, but that one was one of our favorites. We sang it very differently back then, though: "what's love got to doin' it, got to doin' it," banging our heads on the back seat of the car.

I was also very fascinated by lights and the many colors of rainbows, and I loved animals. Some of my fondest memories are of going to my father's job. There was this one location called the Wilderness. At the Wilderness there were tons of farm animals, and in the winter and spring, they housed a few baby chicks. It always interested me how life began and how adorably the babies of any animal adapted to their surroundings. I was about seven or eight, and I remember thinking that those chicks were so cute, and one day I was going to have animals. My interest in animals continued to grow, and anytime there was an event where there were animals, I wanted to attend.

Starting grade school was very challenging, not only because I was taller than my teacher, but also because I had trouble learning in class. My teacher quickly recommended certain classes for me that would be beneficial. After some deeper analysis, it was confirmed that I had dyslexia, which is a learning disability. I had difficulty with my math and reading. In first grade I was held back. I felt like I was a complete failure because all my classmates continued on, but I was left behind. That was the start of my feelings of insufficiency.

I had my math and English lessons in a smaller class off to itself, but I was in a normal setting for other subjects, such as science, which was my favorite. Being in special classes did help me become better at those subjects, but it affected my self-esteem. The other kids called us "slow" and the "retard crew." I remember some days trailing behind my teacher, pretending I did not belong in her class. It was oh, so noticeable that we were her students. Sometimes she would sit in our regular class and hover over us to ensure we were doing things correctly. When it was time to exit, she would proclaim in front of everyone, "My students, follow me," and the four of us would leave with her. Mrs. Klinebacker was an older lady who was really nice and had grayish-blond hair and wore bifocals. She pushed a cart around and walked with a slight limp. I never got used to being a part of this class. For me it was as if I was not normal, but different.

My brother Darnell, on the other hand, was outgoing, funny, very bold, and intelligent. He didn't need the special class. He also made friends rather quickly. I guess you could say that I truly envied him, but he was my brother, and I loved him.

When we got off the school bus, it usually would take us fifteen minutes to get home. Our routine was the same every day. After school we would rush home to watch *He-Man*, *She-Ra*, and *Fat Albert*. Mom would have a snack ready for us, along with a little cup of Kool-Aid to enjoy. Usually, it was a peanut butter and jelly sandwich or bologna and cheese with chips. After snack was over, it was homework and then chore time. Usually, we had to alternate between taking trash out and sweeping. We really did not have a lot of chores. We weren't able to go outside until all the chores were completely finished.

When we went on field trips, my mom made the best lunches. While the others had ham and cheese, we had sloppy joes on toasted bread. I remember the kids all asking, "What did you bring for lunch?" and I had a proud way of saying, "I have sloppy joe and chips." Kids envied that I didn't have the traditional sandwich. Mom made sure everything was neatly tucked away in aluminum foil or ziplock bags.

There were also hard times when we were low on food, and Mom would make sure we ate first. I can recall a few times when Mom would say, "Y'all go ahead and eat. I am fine." After a while, her stomach was growling. I would always say, "Mom, you can have some of mine," and she would always respond, "I am good, baby." That was our mother's love. We never went on welfare, but we did struggle. Sometimes when Dad would be stuck in Maryland because of the weather, Mom would make soups and fried potatoes or rice with butter, milk and sugar. Those were some of the best meals that would fill our bellies and really didn't cost much.

Next door to us were our cousins, and the youngest of them was Alicia. She was a smart, energetic little girl who always seemed to know when we were home. She would come over and play video games and help with the chores, and the best part of her was that she was a girl. It was like having a little sister. Many times when she came around, we would play as if we were fairies flying in the sky, and we'd fold up paper in the shapes of fans and stuff them in the back of our pants. She and I have many great memories of when we hung out.

When the holidays came, we would have loads of food and family around. Christmastime was my favorite time of the year. We would be so eager to see what Santa had brought us that we would tippy toe into the living room every few hours to see if he had come. The first few times, there was nothing in sight, but the last time, the room was hugely overstocked with Christmas gifts. I told my brothers that we should ask Mom and Dad if we could open some of the gifts. Well, the rule was one present until our parents were awake. We were eager to open the one gift, but deciding which one to open was a challenge for us. One year in particular, my brother and I received one of the best gifts: Laser Tag Academy. We chased each other through the house and out the back door and ran amok. Another year we received a Nintendo system. That was one of the best gifts; every kid wanted one. The games that were included were Super Mario Brothers and Duck Hunt. We were addicted to that game, playing for hours at a time, and we even had the adults join in.

I also recall days when Dad would get off work, and Darnell and I would take his blue winter coat and put one arm in each side of the coat and flip over the couch. We lived on the edge. Those were some of the best memories.

As we began to mature, a division started. My brother, well, he was an instant hit and made friends rather quickly, while I, well, not so much. I found out early on that I was different; I didn't fit in.

I was a misfit: tall and underweight and loved to read about science and animals. The first day I knew I was different was when I got called *freakazoid* and *nerd*. I remember it like it was yesterday. I remember my classmates laughing, and so I knew it wasn't anything good. It seemed like the feelings of inadequacy radiated from my pores like sweat on a humid summer's day. I spent an abundance of time reading and writing to express my inner thoughts. There were several occasions that I felt so alone. I can recall my mother telling me, "Go outside and get some sun before you dry up like a raisin." What she started to realize was I hated the outdoors. The sun, heat, bugs…and besides, most kids in my neighborhood seemed to not like me. Kids are cruel, as we all know, but I was not prepared for how they were going to treat me. The name-calling toward me was so consistent, it was as if that was all they knew. Sure, I could have told my mother, but my mother didn't play. Like a female lion protecting her young—that was my mother. In my mind I really didn't want her to go to jail. In my room I felt peace, and I was able to escape the reality of my life. I was different, and there was nothing anyone could say or do that could change this.

Things were made a little better when I started to make friends. I only had a few—Samantha, Jill, Tonya, Sharon, and Tameka—but they were the best. We had good times listening to music, walking around the trailer park, playing video games, and just doing girl stuff. We have many memories of just sitting on the green electric box singing some of the latest hits. We had girl power, and we laughed and joked all the time. We even shared stories about when our periods first started. Sharon and Samantha were sisters, both very pretty, with curly dark brown hair and caramel complexions. Jill and Tameka were the youngest. They were skinny like me, with long jet-black hair. And Tonya was almost my age. She was voluptuous for her age and was ready to fight if someone said the wrong thing to her. I loved my friends; they all were different.

When we started junior high, we noticed a shift in Sharon. She became kind of distant. Whenever the "in" girls were together, they would call her over, and she would always comply and leave us behind. I didn't care for this new Sharon. It was like she was not part of our team anymore, but that's what happens when you go to junior high. So division started slowly, and one by one, my friends started to change. Some even moved away. I remember being so sad the day the sisters left. They were my only best friends. We gave one another hugs and realized that it was really the last day we were going to see one another.

Then at one point, it was just me and Tonya. Tonya was a lot of fun. We had guys chasing us around, but they were mostly chasing Tonya because she was voluptuous and had a beautiful smile. We became really good friends and went on several trips to nature trails and amusement parks. She was the last friend I had, but even that friendship slowly dissolved when one day she broke the news to me that she was moving. I told her, "Really? Wow. It's no one left—everyone's moving." I was sad and angry that they were all moving, and I was still going to be at the same location. It was a Sunday when Tonya moved. Her mother loved me as if I were her own. We said our good-byes, and I even cried a little that day.

During this time I had become rather attached to visiting my grandmother Clara. We had so much fun on our little outings, whether it was going to a thrift store, visiting family, or going out to eat. She wasn't just my grandma; she was my friend.

I was about twelve, and I was old enough to start having pets. I started out with a baby turtle that my grandmother Leana found trying to cross the road. It was so small—just the size of a walnut. I liked it, but I found out early that reptiles weren't my pet of choice. So the next pets I had were fish. I loved fish, the way they seemed to gracefully flow through the water as if they were flying. I remember a few times coming home with about twenty goldfish, and each time, they would die one by one. I didn't have a fish tank; I had a huge container that was used to hold cheese balls. I wasn't that educated about fish until I buried the last of my goldfish. This led me to doing deeper research. I learned everything there was to know about them, from what temperature best suited them to their breeding skills, which I found to be the most interesting. I started breeding fish at thirteen years old, after locating a baby fish in my aquarium. At first I thought it was nothing more than a mosquito larva, but as I looked closer, I realized it was a miniature version of the adult fish. I quickly scooped it out with a fishing net. It didn't live very long, but I was fascinated.

I later became consumed with the magic of life. I studied every type of fish there was. Egg layers, live bearing, bubble-nest builders, salt water, freshwater...you name it, I was reading about it. I was a natural with this newfound hobby. I loved the beautiful colors of fish, and one day, my grandmother bought me a twenty-gallon aquarium. I was so thrilled; I couldn't wait to set it up. I had decided on getting blue rocks and green plants, and the fluorescent light brought all the colors to life. I loved variations in fish types, but I was determined to have some babies. So I always had a male and female and tried to get a fish that was already pregnant. I started out with the ones that seemed to be the easiest: guppies. It was very easy to distinguish when a mother guppy was close to delivery: her stomach would swell to twice the size of her body, and there always was a dark spot near the bottom fin. I have so many great memories of the birth of new babies. It seemed like every month I had a new brood of platies, mollies, and guppies. I had purchased a ten-gallon aquarium to keep the babies safe from their predator parents.

I truly love fish, but I love birds too, and the next thing I knew, Grandma Clara was getting me a parakeet. It was green and yellow. My brother Darnell had one, too, but his was blue and white. They seemed to fight most of the time, but when it was feeding time, they stopped the dispute for the pleasure of consuming all the seeds.

My love for animals didn't stop there either. Easter would come, and Grandma would buy rabbits, and one year she got us all ducks. Well, you can say they were mine, because I paid more attention to them than my brothers did. I remember when she first brought them home; they were in a carton and were so fluffy with soft yellow feathers. Since they needed more space, we left them at our other grandmother's house. She had a basement where the ducklings were kept until they were old enough to explore the outside, and then my auntie Cindy helped me build a pond. She had a broken foot, but that still wasn't enough to stop her. My aunt was so cool; she always let us go outside and play. She liked to explore new things and was always up to doing what our parents wouldn't want to do, like making mud pies or catching lightning bugs. She did it all.

My obsession with animals continued to grow. I had fish, parakeets, ducks, rabbits, cats, hamsters, and dogs. It was like I was the owner of a pet shop.

LESSON 4

FINDING ANYTHING TO HEAL AN OPEN WOUND ISN'T THE BEST THING TO DO

In the fall of 1994, my mother and father's relationship had taken a turn for the worse. They were no longer happy together. They called us all into the living room, sat us down on the solid-wood furniture, and started to discuss the fact that they were splitting up. My brothers and I sat looking at the light-blue carpet and the wood paneling on the walls. I don't know what was going through my brothers' heads, but I knew it wasn't good. Me, well, I just wanted to cry. My family was splitting up. All the great times that we shared were just going to be memories. I held back the tears until I was back in my room. Our parents assured us that they loved us and would always be there for us. They said that we would stay with our father. I remember crying later, feeling alone yet again. I spent countless hours in my room looking out the window. It was a hard time dealing with their separation and the criticism of my peers. My brother Darnell had friends, but at this point, my friends had moved to other parts of Virginia.

During this time, my mother and father both started to connect with others, and so it began. Dad's girlfriend Alice was a short, curvy woman with a quiet demeanor. She had the same complexion as Mom. Mom's boyfriend Jared was about five foot nine, with jet-black hair and the same complexion as Dad. I guess they were OK to just be their other halves, but to see them close to our parents made me sick. It took a while to get acclimated to these two. We tried to get us used to it, but it never felt the same. We just had to accept it. At times it felt as though Alice and Jared were trying to buy us. Well, we all were accepting of the gifts. Not only did we receive gifts, but we also were taken to the skating rink, the movies, and county fairs. We did quite a few of things. It had its pros, but it still didn't match our mom and dad being together.

One cold fall morning, I missed the bus. Actually, I did it on purpose. I hated school, especially middle school, and seventh grade I hated more. It was the last place I wanted to be. I walked slowly to the bus stop, peeked around the corner to see if the bus had left, and saw the big yellow bus pull off. I knew I could go home, turn up the heat, and go to sleep. I thought to myself, this will be a good day.

Trying to avoid being seen, I decided to take the shortcut home, walking through the more wooded area of the trailer park. Then an older man, who was slightly buff with an olive complexion and coal-black curly hair, came through and told me I was cute. I smiled and gave a reserved hi. He responded with "Would you like to come and play some video games?" I hesitated at first, and then I looked back, and there he stood, giving me the attention that no one else was available to give me.

He had a camper that was brown and white and slightly rusty from the rain. It was really cool the way it was set up, looking similar to a little house. I was a little reluctant to climb the stairs, but I did. He made it seem like it was a place of comfort, but I was still a little uncomfortable...and yet I stayed. He said, "Have you ever been kissed before?"

I said, "No, I haven't," looking kind of suspicious as to why he asked. He then leaned in to kiss me. I yanked back really quickly, and he proceeded to do it again. This time I didn't pull back. I wanted for someone to want me, to desire me, and to love me. All I knew was that I was a freak, and no one really wanted me to be around me. Then he leaned all his weight on me while trying to unbuckle his pants. I said, "I got to go home," and his response was "Come here. You're beautiful." He then proceeded to kiss me again. I pulled away, and the more I pulled, the more he pulled it out. It was weird because I felt it was wrong, but it felt good to be wanted. I finally pulled away and ran back home.

When I finally arrived home, I realized I'd been at his house longer than I thought. It was after 3:00 p.m. I ran to the bathroom and jumped in the shower. The sweat and the smell of his Newport cigarettes was so strong it was in my clothes and hair. I washed my body as if there were mud smeared across it that just seemed hard to remove. I felt dirty and nasty, but it was weird because even though I felt that way, I also enjoyed it, mainly because I was desired and not rejected. For about an hour, I stayed in the shower roughly washing my tarnished skin. By this time my brothers were home playing video games, and I just ran into my room and collapsed on my bed.

I realized that someone saw me, someone heard me, and he thought I was beautiful. I didn't appear freakish to him, and I wasn't a weirdo. I was wanted. I started to think about how someone saw me as beautiful. I would spend countless hours recreating that moment in my mind; it was my escape from my reality. After that incident, I wanted it to happen again, but that man moved away with his family. I told myself that one day I would be married to a man who would love me unconditionally. He would be someone who truly thought I was pretty, and we would have two kids and a farm.

During this time I was still dealing with the name-calling. It wasn't just name-calling, though; it was also threats from bullies. Sometimes there were fights. Kids would always try to humiliate me, and even getting on the bus was hard. Seemed like everyone was like, "Don't sit by me." Some even stuck their legs out as if there wasn't any space to sit.

One year, I met a girl who was tall like me, and she had her own vehicle. Her name was Janice. Janice would always ask me if I needed a ride to school. I was so happy that she offered because it was one less day to deal with the stress. We became friends, but she was in her last years of school, and she graduated and moved. Seemed like every friend I had was moving away.

In eighth grade it seemed like things just got worse. I remember one day I was walking home from getting the mail, and the sound of a roaring engine seemed to get louder and louder. I turned around and saw a white vehicle driving erratically and swerving as if to hit me. I quickly jumped into the ditch, dropping all the mail. When I looked up, I saw a car filled with high school students. They began yelling names like *freak*, *nerd*, and *dweeb*. I had every name in the book thrown at me. They drove by laughing as if it was all a game.

I hated my life and wanted so bad for it to be over. Sometimes I would go home and grab a knife and think of ways to end it. When I looked in the mirror, I saw the skinniest, flat-chested, no-butt androgynous girl who was lacking everything. I hated myself, and every time I walked past a mirror, my soul screamed, "Just end it. You will be free!" For some reason I could not actually do it like that. There would be a chance that I would just feel pain and not actually die. I wanted my death to be quick and in my sleep.

LESSON 5

BECOME AWARE OF YOUR PAIN SO
YOU CAN HEAL IT

I t was the summer of 1993, and we noticed that our parents were spending more time together. Could it be that they were reconnecting? The answer was yes. Mom and Dad's love was just that powerful; it was like electricity. By this time I had reached high school and had grown three inches. I towered over most of my teachers and even my high school crush, Kevin. I was extremely thin but big boned. Being a girl at this height and build made me a major target for brutal bullying. Some days were better than others, but when they were at their worst, it was debilitating. I endured everything from name-calling to being told I was the girl who had HIV. Usually, when people don't have anything to talk about, they make things up. I spent a great many of my years in depression, and I did a good job of concealing it.

What I did to deal with some of the criticism was sing. I sang every day on the way to school, after school, and I even auditioned for talent shows. In one of those shows, I came in first place. Music took me away to places and dreams that I wished could have been my reality.

My favorite subjects were English, science, and drama. Those three subjects I excelled in, and in the other ones, my grades were fair. They weren't the best that they could be because I was always made aware that I was different. In class I had to deal with some students always picking me last and then having my teacher sometimes pairing me up with others who really didn't want to be on my team. From the time I entered the school in the morning to the time the day ended, my nerves seemed to always be on the edge. Walking down the hall, I received laughs and name-calling. The rumors continued on and on, until I finally had a breakdown. I remember I was in drama class, and a classmate of mine saw me in tears. She tried to console me and asked what was wrong, and all I could say was that I wanted to die. She replied, "Don't say that! It's going to get better." She was nice, but she didn't understand what I was dealing with: the rumors that I had AIDS or that I had said I was pregnant by a popular school basketball player and how he had confronted me, saying some nasty things. He was popular, and everyone sided with him. I remember I was being so harassed that my mother took me to the sheriff's department to make sure the group of kids couldn't come within so many feet of me. Then when other students got word of it, they all wanted to join forces.

I had dealt with too much, and I really couldn't handle another piece of it. When I looked in the mirror, I hated the way I looked. I was too thin, my shape was nonexistent, and I was not cool. I thought I wasn't supposed to be here, and I had no purpose. I wondered why God didn't help. If God existed, why did he let that kid spit on me when I was in fourth grade? Why did he not stop the bullying? Why didn't he help me? I started to question if there was a God. My spirituality was starting to diminish more and more. I felt there was no way out.

So one evening I decided to end it all. I took a bottle of mixed medicine that a friend gave me. I told her I had a bad headache, and she said her mother had some prescription meds that would help. I had it all mapped out in hopes that it would take me away from the pain that had eaten away at the core of my spirit. I remember looking at myself in the mirror and saying, "No one wants you. It's best you give up now." I took the whole bottle of mixed meds—I had ground them up because I couldn't swallow meds—and lay down on the bed, praying to God to just take me. While the tears ran down my face, I sank into a deeper sleep. A few hours passed, and I awoke from the attempt to resolve my worries. I felt extremely sick and rushed to the bathroom to throw up, but I was still in the land of the living. Why hadn't my plan worked?

Little did I know that my classmate had reported what I had told her to the guidance counselor, who had contacted my mother. It was a week after my suicide attempt that my mother asked me, "What's going on with you?" and I told her what I was feeling. She understood, and she asked, "Why didn't you tell me this sooner?" That evening, my parents contacted local counselors and set up an appointment for me. In counseling I began the process of healing. I started to understand how to move beyond my insecurities to see myself not as others saw me but as something much more beautiful. After some time passed, I decided my sessions had done their work, or at least I thought they had.

It was the fall of 1993, and things started to get better. I began to make new friends, and whenever someone wanted to fight me, I stood my ground. I fought back. One time, this high school girl called me a name, and I said, "Take it back." She responded, "Hell, no," and then she pushed me. I took both hands, and I fought her like she was a punching bag. I vowed to myself I would never let people put their hands on me or make me feel less than. I started gaining respect when I started to respect myself.

Things at home had improved also. Not only were our parents back together, but they had also decided to move us into a single-family home. The two-story house with four bedrooms and three bathrooms sat on a half acre of land. This was a dream come true. We all had our own rooms, there was a big backyard, and the neighbors were great. I no longer had to deal with the long walks home from the bus stop. Things were completely different at our new home—no more fights and arguments just complete bliss.

In my sophomore year, I had already started to make changes. Standing up for myself and finally fighting back became my middle name. The years of accepting what others said were over. I was going to define who I was. I had been in several fights and had people throwing salt on my name. It was complete slander. I wasn't going to be scared any longer. Anyone who came for me would have a fight on their hands—size or sex didn't matter. All I knew was that I'd be dammed if anyone would make me feel as insignificant as I felt before. I was important, and people were going to know it.

That year, I played in a high school production of *The Wizard of Oz*. I starred as the leader of the monkeys. What a role! We danced and danced while I summoned my other friends. It was a beautiful play, and the audience loved it. I realized in that moment that I'd taken a stand for myself. My actions in this play stood for more than a role; they also represented who I was. I had a voice, and I mattered.

Around this time my mother knew that I wanted a dog—a Shih Tzu, to be exact. She found something close, a cocker spaniel named Nya. Her coloring was white, brown, and cream. She was oh, so happy to see us, and I felt the same about her. Nya was my child. I loved her just as if she was my baby. She came to me at the perfect time.

LESSON 6

EVERYTHING HIDDEN SHOWS UP IN ONE WAY OR ANOTHER

It was the beginning of a new year, 1994, when my mom found out she was pregnant with her fourth child. I was so happy I was nearly jumping out of my skin. During my mother's pregnancy, she and I became very close. We spent time every day watching talk shows, and we spent a lot of time in her room watching movies and sharing stories. I started to love the daytime dramas. They were the best. It was kind of fun watching Mom go through the many changes of pregnancy. It was so cool to see her belly grow a little bigger each month.

Things were different for Jarvis, though. He had been the baby for so long that he developed resentment toward this newcomer. He was a little distant, and it took him a while to get used to the fact that there was a new baby coming. It meant he would lose his position as the baby.

At 5:00 a.m. on October 12, Columbus Day, Mom was induced. My father and I helped her along the way. My dad thought he could go grab a bite to eat, and when he returned, they were already setting up for the birth. Dad rushed over to Mom's right side, and

I had the left side, each of us holding one leg and helping her bear down. We encouraged her to push. I also started singing Tina Turner's song "Proud Mary," and I had the nurses laughing. Then I looked down, and there I could see his head cresting. It looked like a grayish tent with wavy hair.

I said, "Mom, I see his head. Oh my goodness, he is coming out!"

The doctors said for her to do a few more pushes and, boom, out came the baby. Dad cut the umbilical cord, and they showed the baby to Mom and then cleaned him up, wrapping him in a blanket and handing him over to Mom. He was adorable, similar to my other little brother. It was one of the most memorable moments and the best things I had ever witnessed. They named him Jacob.

Life changed. I had a new baby brother, and I was about to graduate from high school. I was working at a well-known fast food restaurant, so I had a little income and was able to get my very first TV. I had also finally started to date. My boyfriend's name was Xavier, and he had been a friend of mine for a few years. He was five foot nine, and he had full cheeks and a beard. He was a very handsome guy. My family loved him, and so did I. He gave me some of the best times. We spent several evenings at his parents' house, watching movies and eating dinner. I loved being with him.

I was happy with how things in my life were finally working out. That is, until my boyfriend's behavior started to change. I noticed he did not want me to touch him or get close to him. I asked him, "What's going on? You didn't have a problem before."

His response was "Well, it's hot."

I did not buy this, and he became mad at me and stormed out of my house and started walking home. I cried and said, "No, don't go. We can work it out, whatever it is." He informed me that he had cheated. I broke down and cried. It hurt so badly, but I couldn't end it, so we stayed together. It would take a lot more before I would give Xavier up. He was my first boyfriend, and I loved him.

It wasn't much longer before Xavier broke it off with me, saying I did not trust him, and he could not take it any longer. It was hard dealing with his rejection—he was my first love—but I had to accept it. I wished him the best and kept it moving.

After high school, I went on to work as a general clerk for a well-known insurance company. It was not that bad of a job. I made many acquaintances, and for the first time, I had a strong income coming in, along with great benefits. At the time my vehicle was a tan 1998 Ford Escort. It was a nice vehicle. I remember the day I purchased it. My dad and my mother accompanied me while I looked over several cars, but the '98 Escort stuck out the most. Because I didn't yet have any credit, of course I needed a cosigner to get it. This was the start of my establishing a credit history.

Life was going pretty well, but something was missing. It was great being a general clerk, but it wasn't satisfying. I still had a passion for animals. I had always loved animals and knew I wanted a career in dealing with them. I was also the type of person who always thought about money, so I knew I needed a stepping-stone that would help finance College. I didn't know how I was going to do it, but I knew I had to figure out a plan. One day, my uncle gave me a self-help book written by a well-known author. I knew I had work to do, especially on forgiveness, but how was I going to approach this situation? How could I reach this goal? The questions seemed to flood my brain.

While trying to understand my life and what my next move was, I started hanging out with my coworkers. One night, we decided to go out for drinks, but first we needed some gas. So a few friends and I stopped at a gas station before heading to the club, and there was a group of guys of all different heights, weights, and races.

That was when I first met Eric. It was fall, and the temperature had just started to drop. I noticed this guy watching me. He was tall and kind of heavyset, and he had a nice smile. He said, "Excuse me, miss, may I have your name?"

I told him, "The name is Terri."

He smiled and said, "Nice to meet you. I am Eric. These are my friends." When he went to introduce them, they had all connected with my friends.

We chatted it up for about ten minutes, and then his friend said, "Man, we got to go." Eric asked me for my number, and I gave it without hesitation. I thought he was very cute. He had a nice smile, a nice walk, and he smelled really good, but the one thing that I liked most about him was his sense of humor.

Eric seemed like someone I had known for a few years. We instantly connected, and we talked on the phone every day for two weeks. A few times we decided to meet up for a date, but something always came up, until one night I was totally free, and so we linked up together. At this time Eric informed me that he didn't have any money, so we really couldn't catch a movie or dinner. Well, being me, I said, "It's OK; we can just chill and listen to music." Neither one of us had a lot of money. We ended up meeting up near his house, and I waited for him to come outside. Happy to see him, I quickly sprayed myself with sweet perfume. I saw a tall figure get closer to my vehicle. He was smiling and looking just as good as the first time I saw him. As soon as he got in, Eric gave me a hug. He said, "I know this area where we can just chill and listen to music and look at the stars."

I said, "Sure, let's do it."

So we went back behind where the railroad tracks were down a very dark road. There was an open field. I turned up the music, and we talked a little, and then he kissed me. It was so very sloppy, and I was thinking, wow, this guy can't kiss. The music had started to become very romantic. We continued on kissing, and at this point, the kisses were sweet and gentle. It was nice, but things started to get a little hot and heavy. He began to take his hand and rub it under my shirt and under my bra, and he lifted up my panties. We began to kiss even deeper. This went on for a good twenty minutes, and before we knew it, we had steamed up the windows. We both in that moment wanted to get intimate. I was getting ready to get myself in a position where we could actually go into the act, when I realized, no, we shouldn't do this; we can't do this right now; we have to wait.

He said, "Come on, come on."

I said, "No. I can't."

He said, "Just lay right here. Just lay right here. Let me just get some."

I lay there for a minute, but then I was like, "No, I can't do this. Get off me!"

He held me down, and I wrestled with him, trying to get him off, and then I felt a blunt force going inside me. My eyes welled with tears, and I screamed in pain. I felt my insides ripping and tearing each time he went in. I remember looking out my Escort window screaming. My eyes felt as though they were going to pop out of their sockets. I felt my body swell as he tore into the inside of my body. I told him to stop. I said, "That's enough. Get off me! Get off!" He wouldn't get off me. This man was 150 pounds heavier than me and had a stocky build. It wasn't until minutes later that he finally stopped. He just got out of my car and walked away, leaving me there with blood on the seats and on my clothes.

I went home that night and thought about what had happened to me. I didn't know if I could call it rape at that time because I initially wanted to do it, so I just went home and cleaned myself up. I lay across the bed and called a friend. I said, "I really don't know if that was rape."

He said, "No, it was rape. You need to call the authorities."

I told him, "No. I mean, I don't believe it was. I enjoyed the kissing but not the actual sexual part." He tried to encourage me to go ahead and call the authorities, but I could not and would not. No one knew except a friend whom I had sworn to secrecy. He kept my secret, and I kept moving on with my life as if nothing had happened.

LESSON 7

SOMETIMES WHAT WE THINK IS LONG TERM IS ONLY MEANT FOR THE SHORT TERM

One summer's eve, I was lying on the couch in my mother's living room trying to keep cool with the air conditioning on high and the ceiling fan on full speed. A commercial came on the TV from Heritage Institute. I was amazed at the amount of money I could make—forty-five to sixty-five dollars an hour. Then it hit me. This was my chance to have everything I ever desired, including my dream career of becoming an animal behaviorist. That day, I took the necessary steps to start class to become a licensed massage therapist. My school was located one and a half hours away, and I would have to attend it five days a week, Monday through Friday. This was definitely going to be a challenge for me, going to work and school. I knew that if I truly wanted my dream to be my reality, then the hard work and consistency would be necessary.

The first day being back in school was really challenging for me because I had to release the fears that I had suppressed and deal with them head on. Would it be like before? Would I have to deal with the same issues as before, or would it be different? My first teacher was a very average teacher and didn't really show an interest in her job. I didn't really learn a lot from her, and it wasn't until

I had my second teacher that I began to grasp the proper body mechanics and the information needed. John was an extraordinary teacher; he was passionate about what he was teaching, and you could really tell it. That's when I started to enjoy my massage therapy class. There were all types of people in our class—various ages, cultures, and races. Wow, I miss that crew. I still have fond memories of them.

After the nine months were up, we all got prepared for graduation. Our graduation date was in the fall, October 15, 2005, and it was an unusually hot day. We all gathered in a back room dressed in dark blue robes, all very giddy and excited. Our instructor, John, went over the steps we needed to take to receive our diplomas. As the graduation music was being played, my palms were kind of sweaty, and my knees were slightly buckling. I was nervous because I kept on thinking, I hope I don't fall. There were more than eighty students attending, and each one of the ladies received a flower. When they finally called my name, there was huge applause. I nervously smiled and accepted my diploma. I had finally completed my goal. After the ceremony was over, we all gathered outside to take photos. We all exchanged numbers and said our good-byes. It was difficult because my classmates were like family. They all added a little spice to the classroom, and they will forever be missed.

I had made it up in my head that when I was finished with school, I was going to be making excellent pay, and the next goal was going to be applying for jobs and then going to college. I had applied at a physical therapist's office and started my career as a receptionist/massage therapist. I enjoyed working there. My managers were a husband-and-wife couple who always made me feel like I was part of the family. I stayed employed there for about five months, but I felt that there was something better for me out there. I saw an ad for employment with a day spa. I went for an interview and made sure I was dressed nicely and had a positive attitude. The man who interviewed me was a completely genuine man. He seemed to be very positive and hired me the same day. The first day I was employed at the spa was very exciting. I finally was able to consistently show off what I had learned in school.

I had also started a new relationship. Hakeem a forty two year old, college-educated, five-foot-nine, dark-chocolate man with a body that would make me tremble every time. Hakeem and I had met online four years prior to our actually dating, and we had become good friends. As the years passed, we lost contact, and one day I was scrolling through the dating sites and stumbled across his profile and sent him a message. We instantly connected. I decided to give this a full chance, so I devoted a lot of time to talking with him online, chatting on the phone, and sending love letters.

Our love blossomed over two years, and just like any normal couple, it was time to take the next step—not marriage but moving in. Hakeem drove up from Mississippi, and I had already signed the lease for our new apartment. It was June 25, a hot, humid day, when we finally moved in together. I was so thrilled. He arrived at the time I was leaving for work, so we didn't have time to chat very long. I just gave him the key and a big kiss and headed to work. I was so excited I couldn't contain myself. When I finally arrived back at our apartment, it was 6:00 p.m. I rushed into the room to give him another romantic, tantalizing kiss, and I found him on the computer, exiting from sites he had been on as if he had something to hide. I confronted him about it, and he replied, "It's just some junk I was looking up." I brown bagged his answer and proceeded with my kiss.

As the weeks passed, I would learn more and more about this man whom I loved so dearly. There were letters, text messages, e-mails that I would later find, and even though I would find these, I couldn't let him go. He was my everything. I can recall days when I would wake up with tears and go to bed with tears. I couldn't eat or sleep. I found myself in and out of the hospital, and when I asked Hakeem to take me, he was always "too tired." That was his famous phrase. The intensity of the hurt was far more than what I had experienced as a teenage girl.

One time I decided to forgive him, move forward, and cook a romantic meal. It was steak and gravy with mashed potatoes and collard greens. I had it all so special. I ran out to the store for some special seasonings, and when I arrived home, I stumbled across a receipt. Something told me to examine it further, and to my surprise, it was a phone number. My heart pounded, and my eyes started to well up in tears, because my woman's intuition told me that this was a girl's number that my love had with the intentions of using it for sexual benefits. As my hands were shaking and my palms were sweating, I dialed the number. My fear of what this could be was so very present, but I continued to dial the number. The phone rang three times, and a lady answered. I said, "Hi. I found your number in my home. Do you know Hakeem?"

She replied, "Yes, but we're just friends."

I told her, "It's OK. I am not mad at you but at him." She didn't have any responsibility to me, but my man did. I said, "You know, you can have him. I am done."

I hated the fact that my man was connecting with another person, but this man had a problem that I was sick of. I was tired of the tears, tired of going to work with the look of death on my face. I called Hakeem after talking with her and told him he needed to leave. He begged and pleaded for my love and another chance. I couldn't. Hakeem and I had tried counseling and exercise to change the pattern, but nothing worked. I told him it was over, and I needed to move on. I gave him thirty days to move out, and on the tenth day of his notice, he decided to visit family. It was early Friday morning when Hakeem decided to go visit his family. And that evening, I invited a new guy to my home, and I thought he was a breath of fresh air. He was funny, exciting, and fine as hell. Steve had curly hair and was six feet tall with a sun-kissed caramel complexion.

The weekend was great until there was a knock at the door. I was in the shower at the time, and Steve said, "I think your ex is here."

I almost slipped in the shower trying to get to the door. I frantically threw on some clothes, still wet from the shower and with shampoo still in my hair. I looked a mess. I walked to the door, and there was Hakeem. I said, "What are you doing here?"

He said, "Well, I came back early."

"Why?" I asked.

"Because I wanted to," he said.

I told him, "Look, I have company. So you have to wait until we leave."

I ran back in the house and explained to Steve the whole ordeal. He understood, and we gathered his belongings and walked to the car. As I looked back, I could see Hakeem looking sad and gloomy like he lost his puppy. It was a messed-up situation, but had he treated me right, we would not have been there.

On the drive to drop Steve off, we talked about everything, not just what had happened but our likes, dislikes, hobbies—everything. When I arrived back home, Hakeem expressed that he loved me and wanted to work things out.

I told him, "No. I am seeing someone now."

His response was "Well, he can't love you like I can."

I said, "You're right. I don't want to be loved like that again."

The closer it got to the end of the thirty days, the more he continued to try and win me back. One time he actually asked me to marry him. He had a ring and everything, but it was too late. I had had enough of the depressing feelings, and Steve was looking better and better.

We started a love affair rather quickly. When Steve came around, I would feel excited, and the feeling that a guy as fine as him wanted me just shocked me and fed my self-esteem. He liked me, the skinny girl with a lack of curves; he saw me as beautiful.

Steve was wonderful in my eyes. He captured my attention with his sense of humor and his intelligence. As time passed, the true Steve was revealed to me. Sure, he had the great traits I looked for in a mate, but he also possessed bad ones. Like his addiction to alcohol and marijuana, his lack of stability, and his negative perspective on life. He was an opportunist. He also wasn't worthy of the love that I had given him, but I hung in there for one year. Then, when a job opportunity became available, he was gone with barely a good-bye, and the traces of Steve became a faint memory in my mind.

I moved on, focused on my career, still trying to fill the void that had existed since I was a teen. I tried to fill it with any man who could talk. I settled for anything—part-time men, maintenance men, you know name it. I just wanted and needed to be loved. The feelings were so consistent and persistent; it was my addiction. I didn't even see anything wrong with it.

It was the winter a year after Steve left that he contacted me, asking me if he could crash at my place for a while. I didn't see anything wrong with it, and besides, I needed him just as much as he needed me. We mirrored each other: he had issues from childhood that were very present in our adulthood. I was attaching to him in a deeper way. He was not just great eye candy. He was like me and could relate to me on a deeper level. He knew what it felt like to be alone. Despite what we had gone through, I still held on to him. It was February when Steve moved in with me.

At this time, I no longer had the Escort because of an accident, so I had no means of transportation other than a taxi cab or the bus. I was determined to change this, had saved $1,000, and was ready to get a car. I left with strong intent to come back with a car, and I guess a car is what I got. It took me forty-five minutes to walk to the nearest car dealership. As I walked across the lot, a salesman approached me saying roughly, "Can I help you?"

I responded, "Yes, you may. I am looking for a vehicle."

He said, "Let's see what your credit is like."

When he checked, I was approved for a number of vehicles. There were two that stuck out, and I pointed to this little silver car. It was a 2010 Toyota Yaris. I completed the necessary paperwork, gave him my deposit, and ran out the door. I was so excited to start the car and pull off the lot. I named her Felicity. The car was small but perfect for me. My payments were a little high, but that was OK.

I was so excited, I rushed home to tell Steve, but all he did was say, "That's good." He didn't even come out to see the car. Steve was mad that my life was getting better and, well, his was the same. He said, "You can't expect me to get excited when you know my situation." His situation was that he needed somewhere to go. He couldn't move in with me. I was moving back home to be with my family. This was my chance to break away.

LESSON 8

EVERYONE SERVES A PURPOSE

One summer night, a friend of mine asked me if I would like to join her in going to a club in Washington, DC. I was like, sure, so we got all dolled up and hit the streets of DC. I was excited. The last time I went to DC was for a school field trip to the Smithsonian, but this was different. This time I was going as a woman. I was still a little nervous to get out of my shell, but my friend Cindy coached me.

The club was in a nice location. It was a little dark in parts of the club, so I stood close to the wall looking around for much of the time. Then I noticed this guy who looked like Jon B. He was fine as hell. The crowd was so thick that I didn't get a chance to even get him to see me. So we just left. I told Cindy about him, telling her, "Dag, I wish I had an opportunity with him." Then there he was, walking down the sidewalk by the club with two friends. I said excuse me and hello, but he couldn't hear me over the commotion. Then my friend yelled, "My friend wants to talk to you," and his response was "Where she at?" She pointed to the back seat while I rolled down my windows. The closer he got, the more gorgeous he looked. I told him that he was handsome and proceeded to ask him if I could kiss him. He said sure. This kiss felt good. His

37

lips were cold and wet, but the way he delivered it was magnetic. We exchanged numbers and said our good-byes.

That night I went home and lay across my bed, thinking about the night. The thought of him was paralyzing. When morning came, I sat on my balcony listening to Aretha Franklin's "Day Dreaming."

Our relationship was a slow and progressive one. Edward was Bulgarian and completely different from the rest. He was six foot two and very mature at just twenty-six. Edward had a very strong energy about him. He came into America without a pot to piss in, but he managed to survive through difficulty. He had a past similar to mine, feeling like the biggest nerd in his village and dealing with comments belittling his character. I guess you could say that rather than letting that destroy him, he chose to allow it to fuel him to build his character. Edward and I developed a slow, beautiful relationship. He was the first man who gave me that extra encouragement to be me. I can recall one evening in the summer of 2007 when it was really hot, so I thought, Hey, why don't I put on some shorts? I was joking around and said, "Look at this. I look like a toothpick."

Ed replied, "No, you don't. You look beautiful. Get it!"

So I found a pink shirt to match, and he found a pink hat. I ran to the restroom and changed into the attire. When I stepped foot outside, I felt as though everyone could see me and that they were laughing, but, in fact, they weren't.

That day Edward took me on mini adventure to a park in Alexandria, Virginia, where there were tons of people of all walks of life, races, cultures, and ages. This was the first time I had ever seen that much diversity. Black, white, Hispanic, Russian, Ethiopian, gay, straight…you name it. I loved it! Ed showed how important it was to be different and how you should stand up for what you believe in no matter what. We spent a great deal of time conversing about historical facts and sharing childhood stories.

My relationship with Edward continued to blossom, and I finally decided to introduce him to my family. He was an instant hit. They took to him as if he was already family. Ed was laid back but had a great sense of humor. He loved my family, and they loved him also.

There was someone who was very important to me whom he had to meet, and that was my grandmother Clara. It was the early fall of 2009 when I told my grandmother that I wanted to have a luncheon with her so she could meet Ed. She was thrilled! She said, "Let me meet him." So the following Saturday, we drove down from his apartment to hers. Grandma was all dressed and ready to go when I pulled up at her door at the Meadows, a very nice place for the elderly. There she was, smiling broadly. As soon she got in the car, the first thing she said was "Hi. Nice to meet you. Everybody have their seat belts on?"

I replied, "Yes, Granny," and she started asking Ed questions about me and him.

Ed loved my grandma—she had him cracking up—but who wouldn't love her? Grandma Audrey's spirit lit up any room, and she made friends wherever she went. I remember once when I was a child, we were inside the CVS, and Grandma said very loudly, "This right here I need to get for my granddaughter. She is constipated." I was so embarrassed. I looked away.

At the end of our visit, Grandma gave us a plate of food even though we had just eaten at Old Country Buffet. She always has food, and she always sends a plate or a gift or asks if we need some money. As she walked us out, she gave me a hug and kiss, and she hugged Ed and said to him, "Them hams getting big, aren't they?" She was referring to my legs.

Ed was cheezin'. He said, "Yes, they are, Grandma." We all laughed while walking down the hall. He said, "I love your grandma. She is so funny, and she don't play."

I said, "No, she don't."

He finally met my heart. Grandma gave him the stamp of approval. Full force ahead. The love we shared had blossomed into beautiful love. Ed went everywhere with me, to all my family functions, and he included me in all his affairs also.

The summer of 2010, Edward and I went to Atlantic City for a romantic getaway. We left on a Saturday morning for a trip that was four and a half hours long. It was OK, though; we talked the entire time while viewing the scenic route through Maryland, Delaware, and New Jersey. I felt in that one weekend that I learned more about him than I had ever known. Ed had really had a very difficult life, and our bond was more than just physical; it was emotional and spiritual.

When we finally arrived in Atlantic City, Ed and I checked into our hotel, changed into our beachwear, and proceeded to enjoy Atlantic City's beach. This was the first time I'd been in a bathing suit since I was a child. I was a little nervous because it seemed so foreign to me to be half-naked in public. As I walked to the boardwalk, I wrapped myself in my beach towel. Ed was superexcited, and I was nervous as hell. There were tons of people from all walks of life, and I felt as though everyone was looking at me, but they really weren't. I was still a little self-conscious about my thin build. We finally touched the sand, and I felt free. The water, the breeze, and the sand between my toes all seemed to pull me into a trance of relaxation. We really enjoyed the beach.

That night we returned for some of the nighttime attractions. We walked the entire boardwalk, noticing the fancy hotels and all the little shops along the way. I remember seeing the Ferris wheel and thinking, Oh, that would be cool to ride, and before I could say it, Ed said, "Come on, let's get on this." Once we were on, I wanted to get off. It seemed safer looking from a distance, but it was on the boardwalk over water, and I couldn't swim and was a little afraid of heights. My nerves were completely shaken up, but

Ed comforted me and kissed me and said, "There's something I want to say."

I replied, "You scared, too?"

He laughed. "No. Ty, will you marry me?"

I said, "Yes! Oh yes, I will!" I kissed him and hugged him, and then the cart started to rock. I forgot where I was for a hot second. So I said, "Let's hold our composure until this ride is over. It's scaring the hell out of me."

That year I decided to move in with Ed and two other roommates. I had an interview with another spa that was closer to where I was moving, and at the end of August, I received word that I got the job. I was super thrilled, but it was short lived.

LESSON 9

LIFE'S PURPOSE IS MORE THAN FUNCTIONAL ACTIVITY

It was September 15, 2010, when I started my new job. I was a little nervous and excited to start at a new place, and I was welcomed by everyone. The atmosphere was certainly better than at my previous job. That evening, I went home to get more things straightened out for the move and shared with my family my great experience with the new job. They were all very thrilled for me. Even though the day was amazing, it was also very exhausting. So after I prepped for the next day, I crashed into my bed like a ton of bricks.

That night I awoke to someone banging on the door. It was my brother Jarvis. He had tears running from his eyes, and I said, "What's wrong?" as I hugged him, trying to get him to talk, and then he said, "Grandma died." I instantly ran to the bathroom feeling sick and collapsed to the floor saying no! The tears wouldn't stop. I cried so hard; it felt as though my heart was going to explode. I ran from my room to the porch to the living room and sat with my brother and cried some more. It felt like I was in the worst nightmare, and I just wanted to wake up from it. I couldn't catch my breath. I screamed, "Grandma, no!"

A few hours later, Mom and Dad walked in with her keys and her dog, Brandon. It was real, but I still didn't want to believe it. How and why? Why did God take Grandma? She was the life of the family. She was my friend. How could I go on without Granny? It was going to be a long, grueling process to heal from my grandmother's passing.

That morning my parents stayed in the bed. It was as if a black cloud had covered our family, and there wasn't going to be sunlight for a while. Grandma was an intricate part of our family. She was a grandmother, a mother, a friend, a counselor, a cook, and an angel. No one would ever take her place.

We later started the cleanup process, getting her belongings and cleaning her place. It's hard trying to accept the passing of a loved one. We go through so many different emotions. I had lost my grandfather three years prior to this, and yes, I cried. I even lost cousins, great-grandparents, and uncles, but Grandma was my heart. It was going to take a long time to get back to a place of happiness. I loved this woman so much. I tried to go on and carry her with me in my heart, so I started back at work, but during each massage, I had moments when I broke down. I tried to work as hard as I could to keep my mind busy, but it was just too difficult.

One evening, my mother and I decided to visit some of Grandma's old friends. We had pictures to deliver to some of them also. That evening, as I went to knock on the neighbor's door to drop off a picture, I thought that maybe, just maybe, Grandma could hear me cry. I sat in the hallway and said, "Grandma, I don't know if you can hear me, but I need to know what truly happened." I did not hear anything, but then the temperature in the room slowly dropped, and it was different; it felt as if someone walked by me, bringing cold air. Then I heard Grandma's voice just as clear as day. She said that she had a heart attack and that it was her time to go. She had a message to tell my family. She said, "Tell your mom I appreciate what she did while I was alive and what she has done since my passing, and tell everyone I love them all." I started to cry, and I said, "I love you, Grandma," and she said she loved me, too.

That day it was raining outside, with not a spot of sunlight, but suddenly there was a stream of light shining through the hall window. It was as if God was tryna tell me something. I stood up and walked with my hand stretched as if to grab Grandma's hand and said, "It's OK, Grandma. You can go now. We're going to be OK. Go on up with Grandpa." I said I love you and felt the room warm back up. This experience taught me a lot. Not just to make peace with my grandmother's passing but to grow spiritually. A week after her passing, we held a beautiful ceremony in her honor. We laid her body to rest, but her spirit was like a breeze in the summer, flowing around us and cooling us off.

It was time to move on with life, and so I decided to move in with Ed. It was tough in the beginning, trying to adapt to living with three guys, but we managed. One of the roommates, Jack, was gay and very much a neat person. I loved spending time with him, especially because I didn't know anyone around there. We shared a lot of interests and one movie in particular, *The Notebook*, which made me think about Steve from time to time. The story line mimicked the relationship that I shared with Steve to an extent.

At this time Ed and I had started to have our ups and downs, but mostly downs. One of the issues we faced was the language barrier. Although we understood each other, his friends were another thing because they all spoke Bulgarian. I could see that his friends missed spending time with him, so he and I understood that we should have time with friends and time for each other. This soon became problematic because Ed's friends wanted most of his time, and even though we lived together, it was hard to manage quality time with work and school. Some nights he would stay out until 3:00 a.m., leaving me in the apartment by myself.

As time passed I started to make friends and spend time outside the home also, and that's when I met Shelby. She was one of my coworkers, and she was so pleasant and had a warm smile. Her personality was amazing! She was and is now one of my best friends—kindhearted, spiritual, high spirited, and energetic. She and I became really good friends very quickly. After she explained to me that the author of a few books I was reading was, in fact, the founder of a school she attended, it seemed like it was fate for us to have met.

Shelby had told me about a club called the Bunk. It was one of the happening spots. Everyone who was anyone was there. I had a chance to see famous people very close up. Never in a million years did I expect to see, let alone meet, a celebrity, but I did. My life had started on another miraculous change.

It was the fall of 2010, a few months after the passing of my grandmother, and a change had started within me. You see, Grandma lived on the edge. She said what she felt and did what she wanted. Sometimes when a loved one passes, you tend to grab parts of them. For example, Grandma did the unthinkable, and I did, too. I remember being out with Shelby dancing in the streets with our hands in the air singing a rap artist's song that was one of my grandmother's favorites. I can still hear her sing "weed-awewewdaweweeda" like a cop car. Ha-ha.

Like the snake that sheds its skin or the butterfly that emerges from its cocoon, I was no longer a shy girl but a fly girl. Shelby and I were two peas in a pod. Wherever we went, people knew us. It was like we were celebrities. A lot of the time, we were allowed to get in for free. We were the hype girls. We usually were the ones to get the party started. We shared many long conversations about love, sex, relationships; spirituality…no topic was unavoidable. Shelby became my best friend.

My relationship with Edward slowly dissolved. We got into several fights over some of the pettiest things. One fight was simply over how I cut his hair. It was a pathetic fight, simply stupid. We broke up at least three times, and in between the breakups, I would rekindle my love for Steve.

Even though I knew Steve wasn't who I should have been with, he was who I still loved. My heart was in so much confusion, back and forth between the two of them, until finally I broke it off with Steve. I realized that I hadn't enjoyed my single life, having been in relationship after relationship, and I just wanted to have fun. So I finally cut ties with Steve, and I started to focus on myself and my true desires. I started to look into going back to school for psychology. I wanted to understand my patterns, and I wanted to help others who had similar issues.

During this time, my on-again, off-again relationship with Ed was finally coming to an end also. We had another fight about his hair. The fight wasn't just about his hair, though; it was about his friends and their lack of respect for me and him not showing up the way he should have. It was about four o'clock in the evening when the fight was at its worst. We were yelling and cursing each other with bloody words. I collected all my belongings and ran out of the apartment, saying, "That's it." My car was fully loaded with clothes and items I had purchased. I pulled off and left in a very emotional state.

On my way to my parents', I hit many degrees of traffic. I tried to avoid as much of it as possible, but with the combination of my feelings and my car being overly crowded, I reached down, not looking up, and ran into the back of a stopped car ahead of me. My window shattered, my hood flew up, and the car started to smoke. I panicked, thinking that the car would catch on fire. I tried to get out, but my legs wouldn't budge. So I pulled myself out with my upper body and collapsed on the highway. There I was, lying in the middle of the highway. Luckily, a guardian angel came to my rescue. She was my stand-in mother. She gathered my purse and anything that was needed while the EMTs took me to the nearest hospital.

My knees were in excruciating pain, and I could barely move. They took many X-rays and found no broken bones, but they did find that I suffered from degenerative disk disease. It was not major but rare for my age. I also found out I was allergic to the pain medication morphine; I broke out in hives and had a very intense itch. My mother arrived just as one of the nurses was treating the itch, and one of the EMTs came back with her. Handing me something, she said, "I think you might want this." It was my wig. We laughed and I said, "Wow! You could have thrown that in the trash."

I had lost my vehicle and only had transportation from family to get to and from work. Ed called me later to apologize for the fight. He genuinely felt bad. I told him it was OK. We kept a good friendship, and in the process, he sold me his gray 1998 Honda Civic. It was still in great condition. Things started to gradually get better again. I had a vehicle, and I was back on my feet. I had started making new friends and focusing on rebuilding my life's plan. But just as I thought things were getting better, I was faced with a medical issue.

LESSON 10

DON'T LET THE EXTERIOR BE MORE
IMPORTANT THAN THE HEART

There were fibroid cysts that my gynecologist said needed to be taken care of. This required me to be off from work yet again. I was so tired of always having to take off from work, but what can you do?

The morning of my surgery was very scary. Of course, they walk you through everything. You fill out tons of paper work, and they inform you of what could and couldn't happen. There were three different doctors in and out of my room. My mother and my friend Xavier were there the whole time until it was time to wheel me back. I was petrified. I had never been through anything like this before. My room was extremely cold and cramped, loaded with lots of electronic devices to monitor me. A nurse came in to inform me that it was time to change into a hospital gown with little blue covers for my feet. I asked my mother and friend to step out, and so they did. After I was fully covered, I told them they could reenter. Along with them came the nurse and anesthesiologist, and they hooked me up to several machines and connected me to the IV. They started the anesthesia through the IV. They had explained to me that I would feel really sleepy. I told my mother and Xavier that I loved them, and out I went.

The healing process had taken some time. I found out that I had been born with a low white blood cell count, which made it very easy for me to catch colds and get infections. I was back and forth to the hospital because of an infection at the spot where they removed the growth. I was on so much medication, I was constipated for weeks. I was miserable. My parents and brothers took care of me during the healing stages.

To pass the time, I placed an ad on a dating site, and within weeks I connected with two wonderful guys, Tony and Darius. Tony wasn't my first choice of men, but something about him felt genuine. Now, Darius, he was Italian and black and fine as hell— the kind of guy who looked like he had thousands of women after him. He had a very sensitive side to him that was always making me smile. As I was healing from my surgery, Darius and Tony both comforted me. Tony was always available to go to the doctors' appointments with me, and Darius was the one I spoke to before I went to bed every night. I was drawn to Darius like a child to a candy store. You could say that this was infatuation, but whatever it was, it was taking over. Maybe it was those wonderful dimples or that curly jet-black hair. Mmm! I had been connecting to Tony on a more meaningful level.

I had been conversing with the two for two months and knew it was time to make a decision. I chose Darius, the one who was extremely attractive and charming, and then I had to tell Tony it could not go any further than just friendship. I crushed his heart and felt terrible for doing it. I questioned if I had made the right decision. Did I really choose the right one? Should I break it off with Darius and tell him I made a mistake? I could not.

It had been three months, and my feelings for Darius grew stronger. Before I knew it, we were talking about moving in together. Darius gave me something I hadn't experienced, and that was allowing me to be close with his family. They were all very friendly, and soon not only was I in love with him but also with his family. The relationship progressed into something beautiful. I spent a great deal of time at his home. We both shared stories of our past, and there were nights we spent listening to old-school R&B. Music and candlelight—so romantic. This man truly had my heart wrapped up by his charm and witty sense of humor.

It was November when I realized he was no longer the man I thought he was. He had a string of women both at work and on social media. The signs were there in my face, the red flags were presenting themselves, and yet I ignored each one of them. At the end of November, he told me that he didn't want to string me along, and he thought we should let our relationship go. He broke my heart. I guess what they say is true; what goes around comes around. I learned this very quickly from experience. In some ways I sensed what was later revealed—the fact that Darius was a huge liar and cheater who clearly had issues. He had many of the same qualities as many of my past guys, and I continued to make the same mistake.

Although my personal life was suffering, my career life was taking off. I had been recognized for my consistent clientele, and I received a raise. I found a great deal of happiness in my career. I had made many new friends and new associates.

The early part of spring brought me a friend who came in a different form. He was a shy, handsome guy. He was really quiet and kept to himself most of the time. Peter was a six-foot-tall Caucasian male, athletic, with a beautiful smile and greenish-blue eyes. He was a manager at a local coffee shop. One day as I was leaving to start my journey home, I decided to stop for a cup of coffee. He stopped me and said, "Hey, can you give me a hand massage?" and I replied, "Sure." He was amazed at how his hand felt after a few minutes of my massaging it. He thanked me, and I said he was welcome and went on my way. I didn't think any more of it.

Every time I saw Peter after that, he greeted me with a charming smile. He had spunk in his step. One evening, he asked me if I would walk to his car, and so I did. He revealed to me some things about his painful past, and I shared with him a few things about my past. We became close friends, and I really enjoyed spending time with him. Peter had peacefulness about him; he brought me to a place where all was calm.

He invited me to his family's house, and his mother gladly introduced herself and continued to bring comfort every time we met. His family was very different from what I had expected. They were just a normal, down-to-earth family.

Peter was one of the sweetest guys I had ever met. Every morning, he greeted me with a hug and kiss on my cheek. Then he would make me breakfast, which consisted of brown-sugar bacon and a banana-strawberry shake. Some mornings he would wake me and say, "Hey, let's take a walk on the trail," where we would experience what nature was like. The streams, the lake, and the animals in their natural habitat were simply amazing. The natural sounds of the forest were calming—the tree leaves rubbing on each limb, the frogs, the grasshoppers, the birds chirping, the water flowing through the streams. Peter had something special about him. I felt myself falling for him, but I waited until he fell for me.

One day in particular, Peter grabbed my hand and ushered me downstairs to his basement. He said, "Let's sit on the floor."

I was like, "OK, but why not on the couch?"

He said, "Sweetheart, there's something I want to share with you."

I was still like, "Well, OK, but I still don't see why we can't discuss it on the couch where it's comfortable."

He said, "Come on, sweetheart," and I finally agreed.

When we sat on the plush, carpeted floor, he gazed into my chestnut-brown eyes, and I looked back into his mesmerizing, greenish-gray eyes. Then I felt a spiritual experience I had never felt before; it was as though Jesus were looking through his eyes. There was honesty, a truthfulness that was obvious in his eyes.

Peter said, "I want to share something with you that I don't usually share so soon, but I love you!" My eyes welled with tears, and he said, "Don't cry."

I said, "I can't help it. I felt this a few weeks ago."

"Oh really?"

"Yes," I said.

Our relationship never became sexual; it was solely based on friendship, love, and spirituality, and that I was grateful for. Don't get me wrong, we both wanted to, but it was OK just getting more in touch with other parts of ourselves, which bonded the relationship. Our relationship continued to blossom, but there were reservations because Peter had his own personal issues with his beliefs. He struggled with that, and it became the downfall of our relationship. Peter struggled with finding peace in his life. He came from a family that was very privileged. You could say that Peter was spoiled; he had more advantages than others who were his age. Even I was amazed at how good he had it. He may have had a lot of advantages, but it was really a disadvantage because he truly never knew what it was to struggle financially. His personal development was stunted, but his privileges made him feel that he was better than others in some instances, and this made Peter a loner. He kept to himself a great deal because of his lack of communication skills. He was a nice guy—don't get me wrong—but his outlook on life and people was distorted. I tried to communicate with him, but it would always end in him getting angry and yelling and me walking out. There were even times he would tell me, "Just leave. I don't want you here." That lasted for a week, until finally I gave up on our relationship.

Even after the end of our relationship, we still remained cordial to each other. I was never the type to stay mad forever. We continued being friends, but as usual, like any other relationship I had, this one fizzled out.

I had to focus my attention elsewhere, so I decided to figure out a game plan for my business that was going to help me get to all the goals that I wanted to achieve. I had a vision board, which was one of the ideas I got from reading a self-help book. My main goals were to have a family (a husband and kids), own a house, and own my own business. The business was going to be a wellness center that would help people mentally, physically, emotionally, and spiritually. I wanted to help others get through difficulties with the help of massage, yoga, nutrition, and life coaching. I had a strong desire for this, but how could I help someone else when I was still broken inside? That question was posed to me more than once by family and friends. So I just put it to the back of my mind. That dream wouldn't be able to work until I did the work.

Even though I had changed in unimaginable ways, I still had not broken my habit of choosing mates who were emotionally unavailable, financially or emotionally unstable, or just wanted me for sexual pleasure. What was wrong with me? I needed to heal, I needed to forgive, and most importantly, I needed to love me. So I started doing the work. This time I went to see a counselor to understand my complex pattern. Why was it that I stayed in unhealthy relationships? Because I wasn't healthy emotionally, and I learned to deal with pain by getting into another relationship, one after another. The problem was that I never took the time to get to know these guys. Was I stupid? No. I was not conscious of my behavior. As matter of fact, I didn't see anything wrong with it.

My counselor told me to get into a support group for codependency, and so I did. When I came into the group, I was surrounded by men who were nearly senior citizens and who were all sex addicts. I told the head man that I thought I wasn't in the right place, and he said, "Yes, you are." I listened to these guys as they talked about their addictive patterns of wanting sex, and although I wasn't a sex addict, I did need to break my pattern. I went for one month and decided, Hey, I get the message, but this isn't for me.

I stayed in counseling, and one day the counselor asked me questions about my childhood. I told him about the bullying and how I was suicidal, and then he asked, "Have you ever been molested?"

I told him, "I don't think so. I was kissed by an older man, and he grinded on me."

My counselor became quiet and asked, "How did you feel?"

I responded, "It felt good to be desired."

He said, "Now we are getting somewhere."

The questions continued until I told him about the rape. I started crying because I had never told anyone about it, and all the memories of that night came rushing back up. He handed me a tissue, and I cried like I had never cried before. He told me he wanted to see me twice a month for six months. During this time, my homework was to be serious about my business and my goals that excluded a man.

I was also life coached by my best friend's mother. Mrs. Perry gave me some great tips, all of which helped me. I had started back with my hobby of breeding fish. I began to surround myself with women who looked like me. I cut out pictures of singers and actresses who had similar bone structure and looked similar to me, and I included positive quotes on my vision board. My room was a place that was surrounded by positive affirmations. I started to feel stronger each day, and I tried to do something special for myself as often as possible. I was headed for another change, and it felt good.

My vision for my business started with all the services I wanted to offer. I wanted to provide services that would help others. Whenever I spent any time thinking about my vision, it fueled me to be more proactive in making it a reality. I spent time researching what schools I would attend for life coaching and the best price that would allow me to reach my goal in a reasonable amount of time. I had a difficult time deciding between two schools. The first had been founded by the teacher of a friend of mine, and the second was an online program. Of course, I wanted to attend the school my friend had attended. I needed my own spiritual healing. Well, she was perfect, but I had some challenges, and so I had to go with the latter choice.

LESSON 11

YOUR FINANCIAL FREEDOM MIGHT NOT BE THE SAME AS OTHERS'

In 2013, I became overwhelmed not just with depression but also with financial setbacks. My medical bills had finally caught up with me. I was always trying to get caught up, but the minute I paid one bill, there was another. My previous relationships had left a lasting taste in my mouth, and so had my financial status. I had accumulated mounds and mounds of debt, and it was so overwhelming, I sank more and more into a depressed state. I didn't know where to turn. How could I be so irresponsible and allow myself to get this far in debt? I spent days struggling over how to get out of this catastrophe. I tried paying a little on this bill and a little on this one. I tried Lexington Law financial group. They said they could help, and they did, but I still had payday loans out that were over the top. I felt as though there was nothing I could do other than file bankruptcy, but how could I do such a thing? It would last on my credit for ten years. Bankruptcy was by far the last thing I wanted to do, but I felt it was my last chance to resolve my financial issues.

It was a Monday morning. I had contacted a few lawyers who specifically worked with bankruptcy, and I found one who was very helpful and explained all the steps I would have to take. This included gathering all my bills and getting the names and numbers of all my payday loans and presenting them to him. The fee that was required was $1,500. I told him I could make payments, and he agreed. Each month I would give him as much as I could to get the fee completely paid off. It took me around nine months to get the entire fee paid off. I remember I made my last payment twenty days before Thanksgiving, and I was thinking, Thank you, God, that this is the last payment, and I can resolve my financial issues for good.

During this time, I reconnected with a guy I had briefly chatted with over the phone two years prior. Ben was an attorney. He was a very intelligent, debonair, and well-established man. We had met on a dating site, but the first time we attempted to date, it was bad timing, so we dismissed the possibility of a relationship and became just pen pals. This time he sent me an e-mail saying, "Hey, you. Let's meet up for lunch or something." I replied, "Sure," and so we did.

It was the summer of 2013, a sunny, warm day. We agreed to meet at a well-known fish-and-grill restaurant. When I arrived, I was driving my beat-up Honda Civic that I had purchased from an old boyfriend. I sat in the car, waiting patiently for his phone call, and five minutes later, a text came through stating that he had arrived. So I gathered my purse and keys and proceeded to the parking lot closest to the building. There he was, a handsome, smooth-chocolate-toned man standing six foot five. He said, "Hey," as he greeted me with a hug, and his cologne filled my nose while his arms engulfed my body. It was like a *Waiting to Exhale* moment. As we walked toward the restaurant, I noticed our reflection in the windows. We looked perfect together: he was tall, dark, and handsome, and I was tall but slightly shorter than he was, even with heels on.

The lunch was great. We shared stories about our past relationships and current dates. It was funny because we both were expressing everything about other potential mates, but never once did we initiate anything about each other or express our interest in each other. After dinner he asked if I could help him locate something for his sore throat, so we went to a drug store. While we were there, he said, "So you want to catch a movie?"

I replied, "Yes. I don't have any plans for the day."

Even at the movie, we still avoided discussion of the possibility of our entertaining a relationship. The movie wasn't even important; all I knew was that I loved spending time with Ben. After the movie ended, it was still nice outside; it was warm, and the sun had just started to go down. We said our good-byes and said we would chat again later.

I didn't expect him to call that evening, but he did. You see, Ben was a very persistent man. When he wanted something, he went for it. He asked if I could cook, and I replied, "Of course I can."

He said, "Well, can you cook for me? It's been a long time since I had a home-cooked meal."

So we set up another date and made it happen. It was a hot summer day. When I arrived at Ben's house, I was amazed at how prestigious and elegant the neighborhood was. The lawn was dark green, the trees provided just the right amount of shade, and you could tell that the walkways were new. I rang the doorbell, and seconds later, he arrived looking just as charming as the first time. He greeted me with a friendly hug and then ushered me up the stairs. He gave me a brief tour and ended in his kitchen, where we decided on what we needed to prepare the meal. After shopping for the groceries, I prepared baked chicken, zucchini, and mashed potatoes. While I was preparing the plates, Ben set up a place in the living room where we could enjoy our meal. He also put the DVD *42* on (the story of Jackie Robinson, the first African

American major league baseball player). We sat down, and he said a prayer over the meal. It was surprisingly comforting that he had a respect for God. I remember him saying "Wow" after taking his first bite. "Was this too much to ask for from a woman?"

I replied, "What?"

He said, "A home-cooked meal." He then smiled and said, "Thank you."

After enjoying the soulful meal I had prepared, we lay back on the couch and finished watching the movie. Halfway through, he rested his head in my lap. I was a little nervous but tried to act like everything was fine. He then asked me if I wanted to be his girlfriend. Nervously, I responded by nodding my head and softly saying yes. The excitement I felt was like having twenty kids jumping around inside my head. He then caressed my face with desire in his eyes and passion in his heart and kissed me with the warmest, most comforting kiss I had ever experienced. Ben's hands caressed the curves of my body in a slow, seductive manner. Then he grabbed my hand and he ushered me up to his master bedroom, which was lightly scented with passion fruit and men's cologne. He caressed my body from head to toe and ended with a kiss. The passion had just started to unfold when I said, "You know, let's slow this down a bit."

He was slightly disappointed, but he wasn't angry. He replied, "It's OK. We don't need to rush."

Our feeling was mutual as we slowly proceeded on our exciting, exhilarating, passionate love affair. Ben was more to me than just a fly-by-night or a one-night stand. This man was spiritual, hardworking, creative, spontaneous, and fun. He was a dream! He was always up on current affairs. Every day after work, he had something to discuss. I loved it. Every morning I made sure his breakfast was hot and ready for him, and each morning we had a kiss good-bye. We settled into a very natural routine in which the weekends would come, and we would spend mornings cuddled up on the couch watching movies in our pajamas, or sometimes we'd go out for dinner at a local restaurant and then finish with games on the PlayStation. He was very competitive, just like me. So as long as it was one against one, it was a war house. He would get so upset. I can still remember the look on his face, like a scowling old scrooge. When I would win, I would say things like "Yeah, I got skills! Booyah!" and when he would win, he would say things like "How you like me now?" I would reply, "I like you, but you still don't have skills" and laugh while making my competitive comments.

Our relationship was fun, upbeat, and filled with excitement. It was obvious what the next step was. Ben asked me if I wanted to move in with him, and I replied yes. I had been living with my family for quite some time. How could I tell my mother that I was moving out? Well, I couldn't. I just slowly grabbed a few things at a time and dropped them off at his place, and then one day, I finally sent her a text saying that I was moving out. She was so upset, telling me, "Have you lost your mind? You don't even know him!" This was a spontaneous move on my end, but I felt so strongly about it that I had to do it, so one Saturday I loaded all my belongings in my car and fled for Manassas, Virginia, to be with my love.

Ben welcomed me with excitement and created space not only in his life but also in his home. I remember coming home from work and him always greeting me with a kiss and a gift. I was not used to this kind of treatment. A gift, just because? I could never adapt to it. Where I was from, gifts were only given on birthdays and holidays, not to mention that the guys I'd had prior to Ben were not even raised with that mentality, so it was new for me.

As the relationship progressed, he finally revealed that he was in love with me. He also revealed how certain things had affected him from years ago. When he opened up to me about his past, well, I felt the need to do so also, and I shared with him about my molestation and how I went through a series of guys just trying to find love and that I was filing bankruptcy. His response was at first very understanding but later became very disturbing. He later told me that he could never marry me, and it would just be a friends-with-benefits type of relationship. Well, at that moment I was heartbroken. I thought we could work through anything, but that was not the truth. I loved Ben and was extremely heartbroken. The man whom I had an intense love for had changed from the sweet, debonair, comforting gentleman to become insensitive, critical, and hurtful. I remained living with him in hopes that things would change, but they never did. He'd told me that all we could be was friends, and so that's what we became, but we were still sleeping together. Each time, I hoped that it would bring us closer, but it only solidified that we were just friends with benefits.

I decided that it was time to move on with my life, so I sucked up my pride and called my mother to ask her if she and Dad could come and get me, and so they did. I piled all my belongings into black trash bags and said my good-byes as I walked to the car with my eyes filled with tears and my heart shattered into a million pieces. I felt completely disgraced that I had yet another failed relationship. I thought that love was supposed to last, so why couldn't it last with me? This was a short-lived relationship that started out fast and ended quickly because of the fact that I had filed bankruptcy. The fact that he was dealing with hurt from the past didn't help much. It kept him from giving love another try. In hindsight, I don't regret this relationship because it was by far one of the best ones I had. Ben showed me about class and the importance of current affairs. He also showed me that it was very possible to attract a mate whom I desired. Ben was and will always be special to me, and wherever Ben is, I will always wish him the very best. We just weren't a fit.

LESSON 12

YOUR EMOTIONAL STATE CAN AFFECT YOUR PHYSICAL WELLNESS

It was the fall of 2013 when I started to notice an unusual amount of pain in my body. I wasn't sure what was going on, but my mother, having had many of her own health issues, casually diagnosed me herself. She said, "You might want to get your blood work and see a rheumatologist to ensure it's not anything major."

That November I set up an appointment with a local doctor. When I arrived at the office, I was taken back to consult with a nurse and do the usual routine like weight and height and the regular questionnaire. I'd had blood work a few weeks prior, so there was no need for that. After the nurse had completed the protocol, she assured me that the doctor would be in shortly. I waited patiently, looking around the small office packed with all sorts of things related to bones and diagrams of the human body. Finally, there was a knock at the door, and in walked Dr. Jabbering. He was a short, slightly bald, sixty-something man. He appeared to be Indian, but I wasn't totally sure. He asked me how I was, and I responded with a quick "Not good." He explained that they were going to help me feel good again. Then there was a test that he did on me. He pressed on different regions of my body, and when it was all completed, his answer was determined. I had fibromyalgia.

I instantly went into research mode, trying to learn as much about it as possible. Fibromyalgia is a disorder characterized by widespread pain. It is usually brought on by physical or psychological l trauma. I was somewhat familiar with it because my mother had it as well. Everything added up: all the nights of pain and inability to sleep, difficulty concentrating, the mood swings. It all added up. When I read that trauma is usually the cause, it gave me a flashback to my childhood. The memories of getting teased and tormented, the fights that had been spawned from that, or was it the rape, or maybe it was something that I had suppressed? I really didn't know. The point was that I had a health issue now that I had to learn to deal with. I had missed a few days of work, and things were a little different, especially now that I didn't have Ben in my life. He had provided a distraction from my health and self-esteem issues. I spent a lot of nights driving home in pain physically and mentally. The medication that was prescribed to me was amitriptyline. It's used for fibromyalgia symptoms and depression, which was exactly what I had.

I remember some nights heading from my job—which, by the way, was an hour and a half away—and always listening to slow jams. It is funny how you can turn on the radio, and that one song comes on, and you know every word to it, and then you sing it with such conviction and passion. That's what I did for the remainder of that year.

When New Year's Eve came, I spent it with my mother and father, eating black-eyed peas and cornbread. It is said that black-eyed peas will give you good luck. I don't know if this is true, but it sure tasted good. As the countdown approached, my mother woke me. I sat up in a somewhat relaxed position watching the New Year come in and thinking, this will be my year to shine. I had declared that this was going to be by far a better year than the year before, and I would focus on my business and getting back to me.

In 2014 I was focused on a few goals: I wanted to gain weight, and I wanted to figure out how I was going to go about starting my business. So I purchased some herbal meds on the Internet and went to the bookstore and purchased a book on starting your own business.

Gaining weight was just as difficult as losing weight. I purchased some Ensure drinks and continued to eat roughly four thousand calories a day. My idol for gaining weight was Buffy the Body. She was well known for her fabulous figure. The one thing I loved about her story was that she was just like me; she struggled with her weight, too, and finally reached her goal. I spent hours researching, studying her videos, and working out in an extremely competitive way. By the end of August, I had gained fifteen pounds. I was no longer thin but thick in all the right spots. I loved it. I wore lots of tights and spandex material to show off my new figure. This added weight gave me not only extra self-esteem but a new appreciation for my mother and grandmothers. I had inherited the butt and hips. It was the start to something new.

As far as my business went, well, I had discovered my plan and now things were starting to look better. I had increased my clientele from three to twenty regulars. My side business had started to take off. The money was great. I was still employed at a well-known spa, and things were better financially.

LESSON 13

A BROKEN HEART IS THE ENDING OF ONE EXPERIENCE BUT GIVES BIRTH TO A NEW ONE

It was January 1, 2014, the beginning of another year, but this meant more than just a repeat of the year before. I was preparing to make some radical changes in my life. I had spent too many years financially supporting a man, in and out of hospitals and doctors' offices, all from the agony of the numerous acts of infidelity. I had to experience financial setbacks over and over again to even consider bankruptcy, but here I was, one payment shy of completing the process of eliminating all my financial struggles. I was also dealing with car troubles and a traffic ticket for driving without insurance. My vehicle registration had expired, and my license was suspended. I was no longer able to operate a vehicle. So every other day, I had to have a family member drive me to and from work. I was going to be so excited when I finally paid off my ticket. I felt like a burden having to ask others to give me a ride to work. I had restrictions, a lot of restrictions. January came with great things: I celebrated my thirty-third birthday and completed my bankruptcy filing.

It was cold, gloomy, and rainy day in January when my mother and I attended a meeting in Richmond, Virginia, with my lawyer and three other members of the court. While waiting to hear my name called, I sat among about fifty others who were all looking to rectify their financial matters. My lawyer consulted with me before the proceedings, giving me heads-up about what all was going to take place. When my name was called, I grabbed my important documents and walked slowly down the aisle between the rows of people. As I sat, a court member began the grueling process of going over all my information, making sure all my debt was included. After the meeting was completed, my mother and I walked out of the conference room, and my lawyer gave me instructions on how long it would take before I received my discharge papers. It would take approximately ninety days.

At that time I finally got my traffic ticket paid off and was no longer on suspension. I was able to drive and could get my very first vehicle without a cosigner. I decided on a blue Hyundai Elantra. I remember pulling off the lot in my new car. It was such a liberating feeling. I was no longer restricted by my license or financial burdens. I was finally free. I was doing great. I had been working on my plan to open my business and set out a plan to achieve it. I had spent enough time rescuing men. It was time to rescue myself, to focus on all that I had neglected about me.

One night, I was hanging out with a few coworkers, and we went to a local club. I had given up on finding a mate for love, so I just enjoyed myself. I danced with every guy in the club, having shot after shot. It was a celebration for me. Freedom! The night was young, and the laughs were endless. I was acting like a fool who just won the lottery. The club had a nice turnout.

At the end of the night, my friends and I were getting ready to leave when I noticed this very energetic, skinny, handsome guy. I said, "Hi. What's your name?"

He said, "Denis."

I said, "Can I call you sometime?" I don't know what got into me. Maybe it was the four shots of vodka.

He responded, "Yeah, but don't take my number unless you're going to use it."

I responded, "Yes, I will." I was very playful with Denis.

I texted him the following morning, and we continued to text. Then it led to actual conversations. Two weeks later he asked me out on our first date. When I arrived, he was waiting, standing there with a smile on his face. He greeted me with a hug and a bouquet of red roses. This man was very excited, and so was I. We decided to see *Get Hard* with Kevin Hart and Will Ferrell. When we went into the movie theater, it was completely packed. We searched for seats, and luckily there were two at the far end on the right. We made it just in time. He was a complete gentleman, making sure I picked which seat best suited me and occasionally asking if there was anything I needed. It was funny because when he asked, my response was "No. I don't really like popcorn," and he was like, "Yeah, I want a steak and cheese sub," and I said, "Me, too." We both laughed and turned back to the movie.

When it was all over, we walked back to our cars. We sat in my car for about twenty minutes listening to music, and then he said, "You know what? I feel like dancing."

I responded, "Me, too," and I told him I knew the perfect spot. It was a place where I knew people who had my back and wouldn't let anything happen to me or whoever I was with. I told him, "Don't worry. Nobody going to mess with you." He laughed, and I said OK.

That night, we owned the floor. I didn't know he could dance, but our bodies meshed together like peanut butter and jelly. We danced so well that the floor opened up for us as people made room. The crowd was watching us as if it was the show *Dancing with the Stars*. It was as if I forgot where I was and who was there. All I knew was just me and him.

We had had a few drinks, and I couldn't possibly drive home. He said, "Is it OK if I take you to my spot, because I don't want you to drive down the road this late?"

I said, "Just know I don't play that 'sleep with people on the first night' crap."

And he said, "It's OK. I am a gentleman and wouldn't want it that way."

When we arrived at his apartment, we had to go up one flight of stairs that seemed to take me hour to walk up. He gave me some of his sweat pants and a white T-shirt to sleep in. His room was neatly organized and with a nice blow-up mattress. The room was freezing, and he asked if I needed an extra blanket. I responded yes, and I also reiterated that he wasn't getting any. He said, "No, dear, I totally respect that." What he did give me was a nice, warm embrace.

I felt extremely comfortable, but I still was thinking, I don't have time for this falling-in-love stuff right now. Denis could be a friend, but the more we hung out, the more I realized how much we had in common. We laughed and joked so much that every day was a comedy adventure. In the weeks to come, we would spend more and more time together. I spent three days out of the week with him, sometimes more. I was starting to catch feelings, and so was he. He had introduced me to his family, friends, and coworkers. This man was serious about me and us.

Our bond grew and grew until I noticed his dancing behavior with other women. It was erotic and completely disrespectful. I brought it to his attention, and he responded, "It's not that big of a deal. Relax." He made me feel like I was over thinking and needed to chill, but I couldn't; it really bothered me. We had several arguments about it. Our relationship started to change. Denis would tell me he was busy on days that we normally would spend together, and I felt something but tried to brush it off, considering I had been through my share of a men cheating on me. I did not want to write him off as another guy playing games.

Within a week of our conversation, he told me to come over. It was a Wednesday at the start of the summer of 2014. We had a great night. We made up, and things were going great, or at least I thought they were. He told me that he needed to see his mother Thursday and was very emotional about her going through so much. I felt his pain and told him we could hang out Friday, and so we did. That Friday I noticed his sheets were off the bed, and his blanket was gone also. It seemed suspicious, but I tried to give him the benefit of the doubt. I casually said, "What happened?"

He said, "Just wanted things clean for you."

I said OK, still not believing him 100 percent but trying to not let it get to me.

It was Saturday, the day of my nephew's birthday, and we were setting up for the party and enjoying his birthday. It was a nice warm day, and the energy was all so positive. When we were almost ready to sing "Happy Birthday," I received a call. It was a strange number, and I wasn't going to answer at first, but something told me I needed to. I answered the call with a very hesitant hello. It was a woman, and she said, "You don't know me, but your man is pretending to be single, and he and I have been hooking up for a while." I felt as though someone had punched me in my stomach. I collapsed back on the nearest tree. I felt so sick, and my family was getting ready to sing "Happy Birthday," so I told her I would call her back. The conversation repeated in my head, and I smiled and tried not to cry as I stood there a little shaky and sang "Happy Birthday."

When it was over, I told a relative what happened and walked over to my car where I and this young lady continued our conversation. She went into full detail about their love affair, or so she put it. I told her I wanted to get him for this. We agreed that we would meet up as soon as my nephew's party was over. Since she didn't have a vehicle, I went to the bus station to meet her. We had planned to shock him at his house and blow a flame in his face, make him feel the fear, the hurt, and the pain on a whole other level.

I explained to her what we were going to do. I called him and told him I was at the doctor's for a family member and wanted to know if I could come over for a bit. He said of course. I walked up the stairs and knocked on the door, greeting him with a kiss and acting as if everything was perfectly fine. I told him I had a surprise for him outside in the car. He was so excited, like a kid on Christmas Day. I told him I was going to run to the restroom really quick. While in the bathroom, I texted the other woman to come upstairs and wait outside. The fuel for the fire was loaded and ready for the match. I calmly said, "I am going to get your surprise. Just a minute." His brothers were there also, waiting patiently to see what it was. I slowly opened the door, and there she was, his other woman. His mouth dropped, and his eyes opened wide, as if he saw a ghost. I ran in front of him asking, "Who this is?" I was screaming and cursing, saying, "Why did you do this to me? After confessing my love for you and all the time I invested in you, and you do this to me!" She had her few words, too.

One of the brothers asked if we could take it outside, and so we did. I had held back the tears for as long as I could. "Why did I tell you about my abuse and you sit up here and hurt me like this?"

Denis tried to win me back, grabbing my hand and saying, "I love you."

The other one, Candace, said, "I thought you loved me."

He said, "No, I don't love you. I love her. Don't go, baby."

I gave him a stern look, and in an aggressive scream I said, "Let me go!"

It was too late. I was done with the lies and the fact that he had betrayed me. It was a hard thing to know I had given another man a shot at my heart, and why was I betrayed? I was a very easygoing woman. I cooked, I supported him in his dreams, we had great chemistry, so what was the issue?

You see, what I failed to realize was that, no matter what you do or don't do, people will eventually present their true selves. The lesson I needed to learn was not to see it as the end of the world but another life lesson. Everyone and every event that happens to us is a step to greater understanding of ourselves. When we fully take the time to observe and listen and ask questions, we will see the person for who they really are. My issue was that I went off four dates and concluded that this person was, in fact, the man of my dreams. Little did I know that in my relationships with men, I was falling for their representative and not who they really were. Had I taken the time to fully commit to making a full observation, maybe I could have saved some time, but that wasn't the case. I was still growing and developing into a strong, independent woman.

LESSON 14

SOMETIMES YOU NEED AN ENCORE
OF A LESSON

It was the closing of another relationship, but I still hurt from the one before. I found myself right back at the beginning, and I mean the beginning. Lonely and heartbroken, I ran back into the arms of what I knew, and that was Steve. I hadn't learned what I needed to in order to let him go. This chapter was a lingering one...all the debt that I had accumulated from this relationship, the stress of him treating me as if I wasn't worthy. Why did I want to entertain this relationship? He was my fallback man, or so my mother put it. He didn't cheat, or so I wanted to believe, and he was always available.

One day in early June, I received a phone call from Steve. He said, "I just wanted to say hi and to see how you've been." My response was simple: "I've been doing OK." He asked if he could take me out, and I agreed. It was very easy talking to Steve. I had all this newfound confidence and strength that I did not have the first time, but I was still brokenhearted from the previous relationship.

Our first date was dinner at a Chinese restaurant that we used to go to. He told me how he had cut back on his cigarettes and how he didn't drink as much either. It all seemed to be looking much better than before. He seemed to have matured a lot. Our relationship grew rather quickly. Steve was, in fact, someone still I loved. He promised that things would be different, and I believed him.

Not far into things, he asked me to marry him, and I said yes. I was so excited. I contacted friends and family to tell them the good news. Some were excited, and others weren't. I was thirty-four and wanted kids and a family. That desire really clouded my judgment, even when the first argument started. I was always running Steve to his friend's house to get some green. It was his calming med, and it kept him calm for the most part. We had more disagreements after that, but I brown bagged them and kept it moving. I was determined to make my relationship work.

It was the middle of summer, and things seemed to be leveling out nicely. Then one day at 5:30 a.m., I received a knock on my door. Even though I was in a deep sleep, I instantly had a flashback of when my grandmother passed. This time it was my youngest brother telling me that Mom was downstairs crying. I rushed downstairs to be by her side, hearing the family's cries. I asked my mother what happened, and she said that Tasha had passed. She was my first cousin. I couldn't believe that this actually true. Her passing was completely shocking. In dealing with her passing, I prayed for her children, her husband, her siblings, and her parents. Tasha had a bubbly personality and was always filled with energy.

I told Steve about it, but he was totally disconnected with his feelings, and I needed him to be there. He said wow, and that was it. I was in my feelings because I was thinking, Why is he not being more comforting? Here I was grieving, and he was emotionally unavailable. That night we had another fight, but I still brushed it under the rug and thought about other couples and how they had their share of fights and how I couldn't always run from a relationship when things got bad.

It was the fall of 2015, and we decided to move into an Extended Stay hotel. The Extended Stay had much of what an apartment would have, but it was in a compact space. There was no oven but a stove, no couch but a bed. It was, in fact, rather cute. We knew we needed appliances and utensils, so we decided to go to the most affordable place, and that was the Goodwill. It was kind of fun searching for the necessary items for our home. We didn't need furniture; we had a bed and a chair, and really that was all we needed.

The first night Steve attempted to make stir fry. It wasn't bad, but he thought it wasn't the best. The next day it was my turn, and when I cooked, the meal turned out really well—even Steve thought so. Once he knew this, he expected me to cook. I didn't mind cooking, but this one particular night, I came home exhausted, and I had pulled the meat out to defrost, thinking that he would take the initiative to cook dinner. I said, "So you didn't cook?"

His response was "I thought you would be cooking."

I looked at him like, so you think I am the maid and the cook? I told him, "Next time I have to work and you're home, you cook." He complied.

We settled into our new place and started a regular routine, which I enjoyed. Our time was spent OK, but we never really did anything except watch TV, make love, and make trips to get his green and his booze. I must admit that when Steve was high, he was a much more pleasant person to be around. With Steve I never knew what I was going to get. Some days it was good, some days it was bad, but I was just trying to make my relationship work. I wasn't going to give up. I was going to fight this time around.

It was the fall of 2015, and we decided it was time to move into a real apartment. We searched and searched for different places, and we finally found a place in Manassas, Virginia. It was really nice there. It was kind of pricey but still within our budget. The only thing about it was that we wouldn't be able to move in for another two months. In that time, Steve had transferred to another place as a cook, but he still had his habit; he still liked smoking his weed and felt like drinking. That was his addiction, and just to keep the peace, I was willing to drive him an hour and thirty minutes so that he could get his satisfaction to get it fixed, to feel complete, to feel content, because if he wasn't, he was mean, he was evil, and he had this attitude about him.

Being around Steve slowly started to deteriorate my personality, my sense of humor, my self-love...everything. So many nights when I got off work, I would actually try not to come home because I would have to deal with his fights, his arguments, his bickering, and his complaining. All I wanted was just to leave this guy, but I couldn't. I felt like if I left him and threw in the towel, I would be giving up, and how could I give up on myself and on the love that I thought I had? It's a sad place to be when you want to leave, but you just don't know how to. On my way to work so many mornings, I would ponder how I would leave, but then I would think, how can I leave? How can I abandon the man whom I love so very much? It was hard. Every time I attempted to leave, the thought of abandoning him and leaving him alone frightened me. I had a family, but Steve didn't. He came from a broken family. His father had been murdered, and his mother was nowhere local. How could I leave this man alone? I made excuses for his behavior: he was stressed, he was depressed, he needed medication, he needed me. The next time he would come around, and things would get better. But things didn't get better; they got worse.

Steve was very manipulative. He was good at it. He made me feel like he was a child and I had to take care of him, and at the same time, he beat me up emotionally and made me feel helpless. I was confused. He made me feel low, but I had to make a decision: Did I want to stay in misery, or did I want to be happy? So many nights, I sat there in the shower and cried, wondering when this was going to come to an end. I really cared for him, and I wanted for this to work. Well, he wasn't going to change; it wasn't going to stop, because he didn't see anything wrong with his behavior. He wasn't able to even address that he had a real problem. He suffered from depression, and he was not ready to own that. All he could do was blame others for his predicament and his circumstances. He was not able to look at himself and analyze who he was and why he was doing what he was doing.

I remember one particular night, I was getting off work but was feeling rather tired, and I asked him, "What do you want for dinner?"

He said, "Well, you can go ahead and get something to eat and then just drop me off at the house."

So I did. I went over to the Chinese restaurant and ordered some takeout. It took me about thirty minutes, so I sat in the car and called up a friend, and she said, "Girl, you got to leave him. He's not bringing you happiness. You're always depressed, and he's draining it."

She was right. I decided that it was time for a change. It was time to let this guy go because I'd been holding on to him way too long. The frustration of not getting him to see that he had a problem was detrimental to my health. Whenever anyone would see me, they saw that my face looked like I had been sucked dry. All the hard work and dedication that I had put in was too much, so I had thrown it away for this man. Why was I sitting up here repeating the same behavior? Well, there was a lesson to be learned, and I was going to find out what the lesson was soon enough.

We had decided that we were going to go to counseling. So one Monday evening, we went in for the counseling session, and I told the counselor, "Look, I feel like I can't say what I want to say without him yelling or screaming or elevating his voice to the point where it just makes me feel uncomfortable."

The therapist spoke to Steve and said, "Why do you think she feels this way?"

He responded, "I don't know. She's just overreacting, and it's her, and it's her!"

He was yelling, and his voice was so elevated that the counselor even said, "Lower your voice. Lower your voice."

He said, "Man, I tell you, she just gets hard, just gets so upset, and so she just gets too upset all the time over little things, and you know I'm still up here struggling. I got a job, and she was looking for work, trying to make sure I got money. I got a lot of stuff on my plate."

The counselor was on his side to a degree because he sympathized with the fact that Steve was a man, and he was struggling, trying to make money and all that, but the counselor didn't see is it emotional abuse that I was going through in this relationship with him. Steve never hit me physically, but he hit me emotionally, and it drained me in so many different ways.

When the next Monday arrived, I decided to go visit my mother. Steve said to me, "Where are you going?"

I said, "Well, I'm going to see my mom. I haven't seen her in a while."

He said, "Why didn't you tell me this at first? I could have rode with you. I could have gone over my friend's house."

I said, "Well, I figured you was going to stay at home."

He said, "You've been complaining about me not wanting to do anything with you, so I figured we could do something today, and now you don't want to spend time with me."

The truth of the matter was that I didn't want to spend time with him. I was tired of his attitude, I was tired of his mood swings, I was tired of everything, and so my response to him was "I just want to be alone for a little while."

He said, "Well, go spend time with your mom."

"OK, I will."

"You just get on my f— nerves."

Then I started yelling. I said, "You know what? I'm just tired of this. I'm tired of dealing with this relationship. I'm tired of everything that you're putting me through. I'm stressed out all the time."

"Oh, so you want to break up with me?" he said.

I said, "Yes, I do."

As I approached our room at the Extended Stay, I felt so nervous I was shaking. I got out of the car and ran up the middle section of the building to get to the floor where my room was. When I got in the room, I grabbed my suitcase, grabbed my bag and all my belongings, and I ran toward the elevators. I was shaking. I couldn't believe I was actually doing it. I was leaving him, and I was getting free. Adrenaline was racing through my body. I did not know if I was going to run into him downstairs. I didn't know if he was going to jump in front of me and stop me from leaving, but I knew I had to make this attempt to flee from him, because if I stayed, he was going to kill me—maybe not physically but emotionally.

When I got to the bottom of the staircase, there was a man at the door, and he held the door for me. I rushed to my car, throwing everything on the back seat, and I backed up my vehicle and pulled off. I looked in my rearview mirror, and I could see Steve throwing his hands up in the air like, really? Did you really just leave me?

When I got halfway down the road, I started crying. The tears ran down my face as if it was a torrential rainstorm. The first person I could think of was my mother. I called her up, and I said, "Mom, I did it. I broke up with him. I just couldn't handle it anymore, Mom. I was just so tired of everything he was putting me through, and I just couldn't do it.

My mom said, "It's OK, Terri. Just come on home. Just come on home."

When I walked through the door at my mom's house, she was still in her bed. I came in, and I started crying. "He was supposed to be my husband."

She said, "No, he wasn't."

I went upstairs to my room and unpacked some of my clothes. Then I lay across my bed and cried

I thought about everything that I had with this man and everything that I was working toward, but I thought about all the misery that had occupied my heart. Questions came up in my head. Why was it that I needed to go back to this relationship? What was it about this relationship that had me going back and forth, back and forth, when the truth of the matter was that I needed to heal and be comfortable with being alone?

LESSON 15

YOU MUST REVISIT THE PAST IN ORDER TO HEAL THE ANGUISH

I think I loved Steve for the person he used to be, but I didn't love him for the person he was. Sometimes in relationships, we tend to overlook who the person is because we're so focused on who the person used to be or pretended to be. Steve had his good points—he was intelligent, he was funny—but Steve was also mean and cruel and insensitive. He had two sides to him; it was as if he was Dr. Hurtful and Mr. Kindness. The majority of the time, he was Dr. Hurtful. I hated being in his presence when he was Dr. Hurtful. My nerves were always shaky and on edge. You never knew which mood he was going to be in.

But why did I return to someone like this? Sure, there was love, but love isn't supposed to be this way. I had spent time on healing from the past. I had grown both spiritually and emotionally. Why was it necessary to repeat this relationship? My views on myself were still not quite where they should be. So it was time for me to do more self-reflection and work on loving me. I had to dig back inside myself yet again and do some soul-searching. I had to peel back all the layers. I was that same little girl who went to school and got bullied and was treated like crap, as if I wasn't deserving of love, and then that older gentleman saw me as being beautiful. I had this habit of always chasing a man for validation and to feel complete. I had a bad, habitual way of dealing with my pain. One relationship after another. I'd hear my family and friends say, "Take some time for you," but I wasn't able to. When I was alone, not attached, I felt that my world would come crumbling down. I needed a relationship for all the wrong reasons. A relationship made me feel good about myself. It gave me confidence; it reminded me that I was special, that I had a purpose. But all the time, all I needed was me. How could I break this habit? Well, first I needed to know that I was worthy of much more, not making a man my main source of happiness.

It was January 2016 when I decided that I was going to go on a man vacation, excluding men from my life for a while. I was going to give up men and not focus on any man again for a while, so for Lent (a religious time for sacrifice), I gave men up. I would have to do the work on myself. I had been journaling. I also attended a lot of counseling during this time, trying to understand as much as I could. I learned through counseling that it really was as bad as I thought. I had to work on so many areas of my life. Loving me was the most important one. Forgiveness was another. I had to really let go of past experiences. It was really vital for me to achieve wellness. When I started to examine my life, I had interest, but did I really need a man? No, not to be happy. What I needed was to love me. I thought I did love me; I thought my feelings about myself were clear, that I was beautiful, and that I had overcome the self-hate. The truth was that I did love me, but that love wasn't as strong as it needed to be. I still disliked myself on many different levels, and a man was a distraction from focusing on what I needed to heal. I had to do more work, a lot of work. During this time I worked on forgiveness for the kids who bullied me, the boyfriends who hurt me, and the guy who raped me.

One day, I thought about all the info I had learned from the self-help books. Most of the books focused on how to heal, saying you have to forgive. OK, I was thinking, what do you do to forgive? Well, I had to let it go. The questions continued: How do I let it go? I started brainstorming and realized that a visual was what I had experienced from the abuse of others, so it would take a visual to let it go. Maybe I could get a helium balloon and write the names of all those who had hurt me, or maybe I could just write their names on a piece of paper and bury it. I decided to bury it.

It was hard. I had written their names on a piece of paper, and as I was writing, the memories flooded my mind. When I had written all their names down, I looked them over twice, and one by one, I said, "I forgive..." and named each one individually. "I forgive you kids who hurt me," I said. "I forgive you for the name-calling and the fights. To my ex-boyfriends, I forgive you if you cheated on me or made me feel less than. To my rapist, I forgive you for hurting and trying to instill fear in me." Last, I had to forgive myself for ever thinking that I wasn't worthy of better and acknowledge that I did not deserve any of the pain. That I was perfect just as I was. I wrapped the ceremony up with a single prayer, asking God to watch over me as I walked a path of self-love and self-fulfillment. I asked for his forgiveness for anytime that I didn't ask for his help and didn't have faith in his power.

While I turned over the dirt covering the names, I cried. Feelings I hadn't felt in a while began to emerge: anger, sadness, and pain. I walked away from the grave feeling freer than I had ever been in my life. I buried the past hurt; I let it go visually and emotionally. It no longer was something that was going to hold me hostage. I was no longer a victim. I walked away from the grave crying because I was finally free from that negative attachment. It was time for me to create an environment that loved and supported me in a positive way.

Vision boards were posted all around my room, and I made positive affirmations each morning. I made me a priority. I had decided I needed to accept the fact that I was six foot one and to acknowledge the fact that I have African, Native American, and European heritage. I had to get back to my roots and learn to accept the diversity that ran through my blood. My features were an expression of who I was. My slightly curved and pointed nose reflected my European and African heritage, and my high cheekbones reflected the Cherokee Indian. The caramel complexion was a mixture of African, Cherokee Indian, and European. When it came to my intelligence, well, I had to really understand dyslexia. I had false beliefs about it—like I thought I was stupid when, in fact, I was intelligent. Dyslexia is just a different way of learning. Many famous people, such as Steven Spielberg, Whoopi Goldberg, Magic Johnson and Tom Cruise, could relate to how I felt. In fact, people with dyslexia actually are stronger in other areas.

Soon I was able to realize that being different wasn't a curse but a blessing. I started to look at myself in the mirror and say, "I love you." I'd look at myself from head to toe: my nose, my jaw line, my hands, my legs, and my feet. Doing this on a regular basis helped restore the unconditional love that I was seeking from others. I'd always known that a part of me was missing, and that part was the unconditional love for me. Our society teaches us that if we're different, we're not acceptable. We're told that we need to blend in, but I say blend out. We don't take the time to really acknowledge all the different parts of us that make us who we are—our cultures, ethnic backgrounds, and religions, even down to how we express ourselves through hairstyles and clothes. When I was in grade school, I took everyone's word as my truth. All I could see was that I was different. I felt like I didn't deserve to be here because I wasn't like everyone else. But now as an adult, I think of myself as being exclusively created with a touch of God's love. I see myself as a beautiful woman who was blessed with being different. We are all distinctively designed, and this is a good thing. The moment that we can start to acknowledge the diversity that runs through our blood and see the differences as a blessing rather than a curse, when we can see that there's no culture better than another and no race better than another, that's the moment when we can start to recognize the gift of uniqueness. We need to celebrate being dissimilar and respect it.

I focused on my business. I set long-term goals, and I also thought about all the negativity that I had witnessed on social media, ideas that supported the distorted belief that if you weren't this way, you weren't attractive. It was and still is the view of this world. If someone is different, he or she is unacceptable, so we should remove that person from our space. We all are individually designed and have a purpose, and the moment we start to appreciate that, this world could truly be a better place. The ideas of creating this flooded my mind. I said, "Why don't we have places where people can generate more positivity?" So then I decided to create a wellness group called Wellness and Peace Reinforced. This group would focus on healthy eating and spiritual, financial, environmental, and emotional growth. I was growing not only emotionally but spiritually. I made my best effort to continue to evolve.

LESSON 16

WHEN SOMEONE PASSES, LOOK FOR THE MESSAGE IN THAT LIFE

I was in my last months of my life-coaching course when I received an early-morning call from my mom saying that my aunt was in the hospital. She had had a stroke, and we needed to drive to Richmond. I hung up the phone, and I remember thinking, Oh my gosh, is this really happening? I sat up in my bed and looked around and started to cry. Then I called my job and told them that I wouldn't be able to make it in to work. I got my clothes on and raced downstairs. My grandmother was just pulling up in the yard. It was me, my grandmother, my mother, and my cousin, and it took us approximately one hour and twenty minutes to get to the hospital, though it seemed like more. We talked over and over about what the outcome could be and whether she would make it or not, but who knew? Only God knew.

The whole family walked into the room, and Aunt Cindy was sitting up in bed with her head bandaged all the way around the top. It was so surreal. She had two or three nurses who were just walking out of the room. We tried to chat it up with her, but you could tell that she was a little out of it. I hated to see my aunt like this. She would usually be the one running around the hospital, grabbing gloves and anything that was in her room so that she could take it home and use it another day. But now when we tried to communicate with her, we could tell that she was out of it. She was not her usual self. The doctors explained her condition, what was going on, and the severity of what she had. When she was able to talk and tried to say my name, all she kept on saying was "T-T-T." She wanted to say my name, but she wasn't able to.

We stayed up at the hospital from early morning to late evening. Everyone was exhausted, physically and emotionally, but it was still so unbelievable that she was in this place. I called friends of mine to get their encouragement. It was very difficult to go through this. It seemed like we spent at least five days out of the week at the hospital. It was draining. We all tried to make a joke of this moment, while waiting and waiting to get word from the doctor about her prognosis. It seemed like she was doing better in the beginning. She was talking and sitting up, she was able to know who some of who was in the room, and she was almost able to say your name sometimes. We all were starting to be optimistic about her condition. We kept our faith strong, believing that it all was in God's hands.

Then one day in early summer, we received another call saying that Aunt Cindy had had another stroke, and this one was worse. The doctor said he wanted the family to all come up. We knew this was not good. We walked to a different region of the hospital that was more calm and isolated. The doctor met us and escorted us back to a room that had a homelike feel to it. We all sat down—me and my aunt, uncle, grandmother, cousin, and mom. The room was silent, and then the doctor proceeded with his statement, explaining that Auntie was going to be in a vegetative state for the remainder of her life and eventually things would start to shut down. He asked my grandmother what she wanted. It was hard for Grandma to say. She had lost three other children, and this was the youngest one still living. My cousin was not there to hear any of this; she had to leave. My grandmother finally came to the harsh reality that if and when Auntie stopped breathing, she didn't want her hanging on by the help of a machine. We all sat in the room brokenhearted, each having our own way of dealing with the news. Everyone felt drained and depressed.

That evening, we returned home to inform other relatives about this. You see, my grandmother, my cousin Denise, and I had a different outlook on the whole situation. We were still thinking that Aunt Cindy could come out of this on top. Denise had a strong belief, and I believed in the laws of attraction and the power of prayer. We saw this as being just a way to test our faith. Our other family members had a more realistic view. It wasn't that they didn't want to see her make it; they just heard what the doctors said but they still hoped for the best.

During the weeks that followed, we spent countless hours calling nursing homes to find one that would be a good fit for her. We found some that were complete nightmares, looking like something from a scary movie. We finally found one with all that she needed, and it was closer to home. It would be easy for us to access this one, and even better for me, considering it was on my way home.

During this time, I tried to keep myself motivated. It was time to take the exam that would determine if I could remember all that I had learned. I explained to my mother and brother that I was getting ready to take the exam. I was nervous, but I studied a lot, so I was prepared. When I signed in to the web address to take my exam, my nerves were a mess, my fingers were shaking, and my palms were sweaty. Once I completed one portion, there was another they wanted for you to complete, an essay on life coaching and how it would benefit someone else. I was actually confident in this portion. The whole test took me an hour. The first portion gave you a grade right away, but the second gave you confirmation the next day. I was so thrilled afterward, I had to tell everyone who knew me. I finally completed the training! I received my certificate after just three days. I was at a loss for words because I was just that happy.

It was late summer and approaching was my aunt's birthday. She was still in her forties. Aunt Cindy was looking better; her skin was really light, and she seemed to have more color to her skin. My grandmother and I cleaned her up, washing her hands and feet, and then I painted her nails a reddish-burgundy color. It looked nice on her. A week later we came back to sing "Happy Birthday" to her. Even though she couldn't respond, we knew she could hear us. There was a moment when we would see her either move her lip or blink her eyes. It was her way of saying, "I hear you." It still was not the aunt, sister, daughter, and cousin that we knew though. Auntie was just as energetic as my grandmother Clara was. Their souls were so big that as soon as they entered the room, it was lit up.

We were still hoping for a good outcome, until another morning phone call put to rest all the hope that she would come out of this OK. One of the nursing home's nurses notified my mother that Aunt Cindy had expired that morning. The way it was said, it was as if she were just a rotten can of milk. Where was the decency and delivering the news with a little compassion? I shed a few tears after my mom broke the news, and I called my job to inform them of my aunt's passing. After we got ourselves together, we drove to one of the people who would take it the hardest, my grandmother. By the time we arrived at the apartment and were walking through the hall, we could hear a mother's pain. It was one of the saddest moments. She explained that the nursing home just contacted her. Trying to comfort her, we held Grandma and cried together. Mom had notified Cousin Denice. She and Auntie were close like sisters, and she took it very hard also. As soon as she came in, she collapsed into Grandma's arms along with Mom.

It was a difficult time for us, and we had to start planning Aunt Cindy's home-going service. When my Aunt Cindy passed, it was a very sad day, but it also was a nice day. We had an opportunity to get together and rejoice in the life of our Cindy. She had a heart that was big and caring, and she always made you laugh with her silly antics. All I know is that the day of her service was beautiful. Our whole entire family was dressed in blue and black, and a few of us had blue roses attached to our shirts. I remember in one part of the funeral, my mother and other relatives stood up and sang one of Cindy's favorite songs. It was a fun time, and they were laughing. Even though we were hurting, we were rejoicing in her life and her remembrance. After it was over, the preacher asked if there was anyone who wanted to come on up and say their last good-byes. For me, even though I was saying good-bye to Aunt Roxanna's body, I wasn't saying good-bye to her spirit. Even though she had transitioned, she was still around us.

After the funeral was over, there was the repast. We went down to the basement, and there was so much food—I mean, all types of this and all types of that. And, of course, I'd made my corn pudding, which I knew was good. We had an opportunity to engage with one another, to talk, to remember, and to catch up on old times. I spent a lot of time walking back and forth, making sure that I took a picture of everyone. We were in a small section of the church, but it was just enough to fit a family. After it was over, I remember my aunt, my cousins, and I headed back to the house to play music in remembrance of our Cindy. We pulled up in the yard, and the family was in the house still changing into their regular clothes, but then we were outside jamming in the parking lot. We had the music so loud, but we were having a good time, and I mean, we danced. Later on that day, a few other relatives came by, and we went outside, had a few drinks, and just talked about all kinds of subjects, especially Aunt Cindy.

The message that I received from her life was to take care of the body you are given. Tomorrow is not promised, so forgive and move on. We did it up for our Cindy. She was special, and I have a ton of memories that I'll never forget about this woman.

LESSON 17

WHEN YOU LOVE YOURSELF, YOU MAKE BETTER DECISIONS

After doing the work on myself, I decided that it was time for me to venture back out and try my luck at finding love again. So I thought of all the dating sites I had tried in the past and how the end results never worked out. Then a coworker recommended that I try this app on which, when looking for a mate, you simply swipe right for yes and left for no, and if you match with someone, then it will tell you that you have a match. I had heard of this app from others. Seemed to be something to at least give a try. In the first few minutes, I connected with a few guys, and in the next hour, there were twenty. The connections continued on, and then this one guy in particular hit me up. He was tall and a huge animal lover. In fact, he had a few pets himself. I hadn't dated a guy like him before. He had a great sense of humor and was very attractive. He was six foot nine and had an olive complexion with a jet-black mustache and goatee.

Our first date was a movie date, very simple and nice. After the movie was over, we shared some time chatting in my car, listening to old-school R&B music. He played a song that made him think of me. Then we shared a passionate kiss that had my lips quivering.

It felt great to be kissed in the way he did it. I told him, "Wow, that was great," and he agreed that it was.

We both wanted to spend more time with each other, but we knew it was time to wrap it up. So he said, "Can I get a hug before you leave?"

I responded, "Sure."

When I got out of the car, he looked at me and said, "Wait, let's take a picture to show our kids one day." I smiled and leaned in closer to his chest, and he took the picture. Then he gave me a warm kiss good-bye. Less than five minutes later, he sent me a text telling me he wanted to see me the next Monday. I had a dentist appointment, so it was perfect timing.

That Monday after my appointment, I texted him, notifying him that I was in the area. He responded, "Great! Here is my address." When I arrived, I found that his place was in a large field with plenty of land. He had plenty of space to have animals. The ones that he did have were mostly farm animals. Stephan was waiting outside, feeding the animals. I was so excited to see him; I couldn't get out of the car fast enough. As soon as I saw him, I kissed him. He then ushered me into his home and asked me if I would like some refreshments. Well, I said yes, of course. In our conversations, animals seemed to be our favorite subject.

The relationship seemed to progress nice and slowly. Each time we met up, it was like the first time. We acted like two giddy kids ready to go to the beach. I started to develop feelings for Stephan after a month. I was trying to be cautious with my heart, but I could not resist that smile. He seemed as if he genuinely liked being around me. For the first month, we saw each other every day. I fell more and more for him. His sarcastic ways were like lingering male cologne that seemed to just put me in a trance.

When we reached the second month, he seemed to be very busy. It seemed as if he was more and more unavailable. I respected it at first because he had work that consumed a lot of his time. Then it seemed that he had time for everything else except me. I just felt that he did not make me a priority, and then I brought it to his attention. I explained to him how I felt, and he promised that things would get better, so I waited to give him a chance, but after another month, I had had enough. I broke it off. I explained to him that if he really wanted me, he would create time and space for me. It hurt for a little while, but I just couldn't deal with this. I felt that Stephan was sweet and kind, but he had this habit of not returning my phone calls or being so consumed at work that he never made time for me. I had done self-renovations and worked on loving myself, so it came very easily to simply say, "No, this isn't for me." So I continued on. Stephan was a cool guy. Was he right for me in some ways? Yes, but I could not settle for good enough. Time was important for me, and I believed in my heart that if someone really wants you in their life, you won't have to struggle for a position in it. I had expectations, and there was nothing wrong with having them. When you treasure yourself, settling for anything is not an option. I realized I was working toward happiness, and any person who didn't bring that into my life, who brought me misery, who brought me pain, or who did not turn out to be the type of guy I was looking for...well, it was time for me to let him go. My days of holding on to an unhealthy relationship were a thing of the past. I couldn't, and I wouldn't. I want more out of a man, like being goal and family oriented, spiritual, and faithful and having a great sense of humor—a man who is emotionally and financially stable. I want someone who complements the woman I am today and not the woman I used to be. Now when I choose a mate, it won't be for validation but for companionship.

Every experience we've ever had has taught us valuable lessons. It's up to us to choose whether to listen to the lesson that's being revealed. In June 2016, I passed my life-coaching exam and became a certified life coach. When I was younger, I questioned why God wasn't there for me, but he *was* there. I now know what my purpose was and is. It was fate that I became a massage therapist and then a life coach, and it was destiny for me to tell my story. My purpose has always been to help others.

LESSON 18

SOMETIMES THE REWARD IS NOT A MEDAL OR A TROPHY BUT THE FEELING YOU GET FROM HELPING OTHERS

Becoming a life coach was not something I instantly thought I would do. I had been a massage therapist for eleven years and found great fulfillment in relieving others. In the process of helping others physically, sometimes clients come in with not just physical issues but also emotional issues, and as I said in a previous chapter, your emotional can manifest itself in your physical. And although I was not a psychologist, I could help others as best as I knew how.

I remember my first client. Our first meeting involved my understanding what she needed my help with. She had a background similar to mine and was in the early stages of figuring out which path she should take. After careful analysis, I realized there was some hidden pain she had not dealt with. I directed her to see someone about those hidden issues. I explained to her that it wasn't until I was able to discover my pain and its origin that I was able to heal. During her counseling, she still remained in contact with me, sharing numerous stories, and we both shed lots of tears. I bonded with her like a little sister. We did exercises that involved her putting focus on her career and healing the pain that had blocked her growth. Each week, I contacted her and gave her my e-mail just in case she needed some extra help through the week. In the process of counseling and seeing me, she was able to break free from the shackles that had held her back from her own goals. We discovered what her setbacks were and other approaches she could take that would be of great value. It took about two months, then one day she said, "Ms. Barnes, thank you for helping me understand myself and figure out my direction, but I think it's about time for me to end my sessions with you." I was neither sad nor disappointed but very proud. I responded, "It's OK! You have made great progress, and be proud of yourself. It's been a pleasure working with you, and I am sure you're going achieve all your goals." This young lady later referred two friends, who soon became my clients.

One of the best lessons I learned from life coaching and being a massage therapist is that the reward is not necessarily what you think it is. Being in service for more than twenty years, I realize that when someone adds a gratuity, it's saying thank you without saying it. Sometimes it's the person saying, "Thank you; you don't know how much you truly helped me," or "Wow! That made my day." Giving to someone with the intention of making him or her smile and to bring joy is truly the reward.

There is so much we can learn from others, like the lady in the supermarket waiting patiently for the cashier to ring her up who starts a random conversation with you or the man who holds the door for you or a positive message on social media. We are all in this thing called life together. We should spread loving acts of the kindness, learn to embrace our differences, and to give and receive the love that God has already shown us.

CPSIA information can be obtained
at www.ICGtesting.com
Printed in the USA
LVOW11s0814170517
534806LV00001B/273/P